Gourmet Garnishes

Gourmet Garnishes

Creative Ways to Dress Up Your Food

Mickey Baskett

Sterling Publishing Co., Inc.
New York

Prolific Impressions Production Staff:
Editor in Chief: Mickey Baskett
Copy Editor: Phyllis Mueller
Computer Graphics: Karen Turpin
Styling: Lenos Key
Photography: Jerry Mucklow, Joel Tressler
Administration: Jim Baskett

Library of Congress Cataloging-in-Publication Data

Baskett, Mickey.
  Gourmet garnishes : creative ways to dress up your food / Mickey Baskett ;
      photography: Jerry Mucklow, Joel Tressler.
      p. cm.
  Includes index.
  ISBN 1-4027-1468-8
  1. Garnishes (Cookery)   I. Title.
TX740.5.B37 2006
641.8'1--dc22
                                                          2005023515

10 9 8 7 6 5 4 3 2 1

Published by Sterling Publishing Co., Inc.
387 Park Avenue South, New York, N.Y. 10016
© 2006 by Prolific Impressions, Inc.
Produced by Prolific Impressions, Inc.
160 South Candler St., Decatur, GA 30030
Distributed in Canada by Sterling Publishing
c/o Canadian Manda Group, 165 Dufferin Street
Toronto, Ontario, Canada M6K 3H6
Distributed in the United Kingdom by GMC Distribution Services,
Castle Place, 166 High Street, Lewes, East Sussex, England BN7 1XU
Distributed in Australia by Capricorn Link (Australia) Pty. Ltd.
P.O. Box 704, Windsor, NSW 2756 Australia

Printed in China

Sterling ISBN-13: 978-1-4027-1468-9
       ISBN-10: 1-4027-1468-8

For information about custom editions, special sales, premium and corporate purchases, please contact Sterling Special Sales Department at 800-805-5489 or specialsales@sterlingpub.com.

I dedicate this book . . .

    to my mother and father, Flora and Michael Kadar, who introduced me to food that nurtured my body and soul. My father taught me how to grow food, how to enjoy it, and how to be creative with it. My mother taught me how to prepare it. They both gave me an appreciation of the foods from our Romanian heritage and helped me have an understanding of the important role food plays in keeping family traditions alive.

    to my husband, Jim; daughter, Miche; and son-in-law, Jonathan who always seem to love the food I put before them. How fulfilling it is to cook for them.

    and, to my grand boys, Earl and J.D., to whom I hope to pass on my love and knowledge of food.

CONTENTS

Simple Techniques
Add Elegance to Meals at Home

There is no doubt that a large part of our enjoyment of food comes from the way food looks. Attractive garnishes play an important role in the preparation and serving of food, elevating ordinary to elegant and mundane to magnificent. Because we eat first with our eyes, the way food is visually presented contributes to our perceptions about it.

If you think garnishes are too difficult or too much trouble, think again. This book is a practical guide for food arrangement and decoration. It shows you, step-by-step, techniques professional chefs use to make food beautiful and appealing. Although there's not a chapter devoted to time-consuming vegetable carving, there is no skimping on information – you'll find a wealth of ideas for quick, easy, and creative embellishing techniques any home cook can master.

From roses of smoked salmon on an appetizer platter to vegetable confetti decorating the plates of a main course to chocolate leaves adorning a layer cake dessert, the garnishes presented are as mouth-watering as they are beautiful. Precise instructions are accompanied by more than 100 photos, easy recipes, and practical serving suggestions.

The information is provided with a sensibility for freshness and simplicity. Fresh, flavorful foods benefit from minimal preparation and fresh, simple garnishes. Chopped fresh herbs, sprinkled spices, citrus twists, or butter curls can make your plates exciting and inviting. More than mere decorations, the garnishes presented are fresh, easy to find, colorful, and delicious to eat.

1
Basic Rules for Garnishing Food

Garnishes are the artistic, individual, creative flair you can give your cuisine. An effective garnish is the touch that sets off the food and tantalizes the eye. It's like confetti – festive, colorful, and decorative.

Tastefully garnished, your signature dishes will reflect your personal style. Imagination and creativity are the key ingredients to this art. Like other art forms, there are guidelines to assist your artistic pursuit.

Rule 1

Garnishes must be edible.

A garnish should be something delicious to eat, not a useless decoration. Plastic figures, vines, inedible flowers, silk flowers, paper decorations, and the like have no place on a plate of food that people are going to eat. When using flowers to decorate a plate, be sure they are edible. (The "Edible Flowers" chapter includes guidelines for choosing flower garnishes.)

The one exception I sometimes make to this rule is decorations on a cake – candles, novelty items, ribbons, and other inedible decorations can be used on celebratory cakes. They should, however, be removed before the cake is sliced, and inedible decorations should never be placed on the plate on which the cake is served to a guest.

Rule 2

Garnishes should be quick and easy.

A garnish shouldn't take more time to create than the food it accompanies. Elegant garnishes are not hard to master. With the confidence gained from knowledge and practice, you can garnish any dish, from soup to dessert, in just a few seconds.

Most home cooks don't have time to carve vegetables in the shapes of swans and dragons and shape fruit into a school of fish or white cranes. These types of artful, time-consuming garnishes are more suitable for banquets and state dinners. But artfully swirled sauces, a nicely placed herb sprig, a frizzle of shredded potatoes, or a simple twisted lemon slice can add color, contrast, and a zing of flavor to everyday meals.

Rule 3
The garnish should enhance the flavor of the food.

A garnish should be part of the taste of the food. If you wouldn't use the food in the dish itself, don't use it as a garnish.

Be sure your garnishes are fresh and tasty. Always use fresh herbs, not dried ones. Lifeless, wilted vegetables and fruits detract from the appearance and flavor of your food. Items that are very salty, such as capers or anchovies, should be used sparingly.

Make the garnish count. A flavorful Bearnaise sauce spooned over a sizzling steak is a classic example of an appropriate garnish. A drizzle of olive oil on a round of goat cheese is enticing and enhances the flavor.

Rule 4
Garnishes should be appropriate to the type of food being garnished.

A dish and its decoration should harmonize and complement each other. Generally, fruits garnish fruit dishes and desserts; vegetables garnish vegetable dishes and meats. Chopped herbs can complement a meat dish, while a ring of lemon slices enhances seafood dishes. Today many chefs are pushing the boundaries of this guideline. I have seen ice cream sprinkled with black pepper, blackberries on broiled fish. This is great for restaurants – but sometimes doesn't work in a home kitchen.

Take a cue from the recipe. To be absolutely sure the garnish is appropriate, garnish the dish with one (or more) of its ingredients. For example, when making guacamole, save some sprigs of fresh cilantro and a slice of lime for garnishes. Or, if your meal contains mushrooms, save a fresh mushroom to slice into a fan for a garnish.

Use garnishes to help diners identify foods. A candied carrot curl atop a puddle of orange puree in a soup plate, for example, informs diners that they are about to eat carrot soup.

Rule 5

Garnishes should add color and contrast to food.

Foods look brighter and more appetizing when they are enhanced with garnishes in contrasting colors. A casserole topped with brown bread crumbs becomes much more appealing with the addition of a sprinkling of chopped red peppers and basil. A bright red raspberry atop a chocolate brownie looks too good not to eat.

When green is needed, use cucumbers, chives, scallions, sprigs of herbs, lettuces, and a variety of greens. Carrots and oranges are bright colors that contrast with the cool greens of salads. The bright red tones of tomatoes, red peppers, and beets look great with dark meats or white foods. Even humble scrambled eggs can be elevated to gourmet status when adorned with a zigzag of roasted red pepper coulis. Think color when you're choosing a garnish, but don't overdo. Three to four colors on a plate is enough.

Rule 6

Consider the size and proportion of the garnish.

The size and shape of the garnish should be in proportion to the size of the food being decorated. A garnish should make the food more attractive, not hide it. A dainty canape needs a tiny spring of herb, not a bundle.

Garnishes should look neat, not sloppy, with the lines and cuts well-defined. Likewise, consider the size and proportion of a plate, as well as its color. Odd numbers seem to work better than even numbers – three sprigs of rosemary look better than four.

Rule 7

Keep it simple.

Often the simplest garnishes are the most elegant. Food is naturally beautiful and appealing – don't overpower it with excessive decoration. Complicated or messy constructions often detract from the beauty and enjoyment of the dish. Let the beauty of the food shine through.

Exercise restraint. A perfectly fresh, well-placed sprig of fennel or cilantro is better than a tangled handful of wilted parsley plopped on the plate.

2
Garnishing Tools

It may surprise you to learn that you probably have all the tools you need in your kitchen drawers. Really! With a few sharp knives and a vegetable peeler, you could do most any garnish in this book. But because gadgets are so much fun to collect and use, I have included a few specialty tools that will make certain garnishing techniques easier. First, the basics.

Knives

Invest in good quality stainless steel or carbon steel knives. They will last for many years if you take care of them. Have them professionally sharpened at least once a year. (Between sharpenings you can use a steel to refine the edges.) **Never** put your sharp knives in the dishwasher or leave them soaking in water. Wash and dry them after each use. Place them in a wooden knife block or attach them to a knife magnet. Don't store them in a drawer – bumping up against each other and other items in the drawer will nick and mar their sharp edges.

Four essential knives:
- **Paring Knife:** This small knife can be used to peel and trim fruits and vegetables.

- **Chef's Knife:** Also called a cook's knife, this knife is used for chopping. A variety of sizes are available. Find one that suits you for weight, balance, and size.

- **Slicing Knife or Utility Knife:** This knife is used to slice and chop.

- **Serrated Knife:** This knife can easily slice bread paper thin. It's also great for cutting cakes and other pastries. The one vegetable I use it to slice is tomatoes. Use a short sawing motion for best results.

Pictured left to right: Kitchen scissors, paring knife, serrated knife, slicing knife, and chef's knife on a plastic cutting board.

Cutting Board

A cutting board is essential for protecting your countertops, but the type of material you choose is a matter of personal preference. I don't recommend glass or stone slabs as cutting boards, however, because they will dull your knives.

Wooden cutting boards are always a good choice. They won't dull your knife blades, they're somewhat stain resistant, and they're aesthetically appealing. The new bamboo cutting boards are very hard and resist stains even better than hardwood boards. You must be sure to thoroughly clean and disinfect wooden boards if you use them for cutting raw meats or seafood.

Plastic cutting boards are available in a variety of colors and can be washed in a dishwasher. There is a composite material that is very hard and resistant to stains and cuts.

Kitchen Scissors

Most cooks cannot do without their kitchen scissors. They can be used for cutting herbs, fruits, and vegetables; and for sectioning meat and fowl. Scissors are particularly useful for snipping chives.

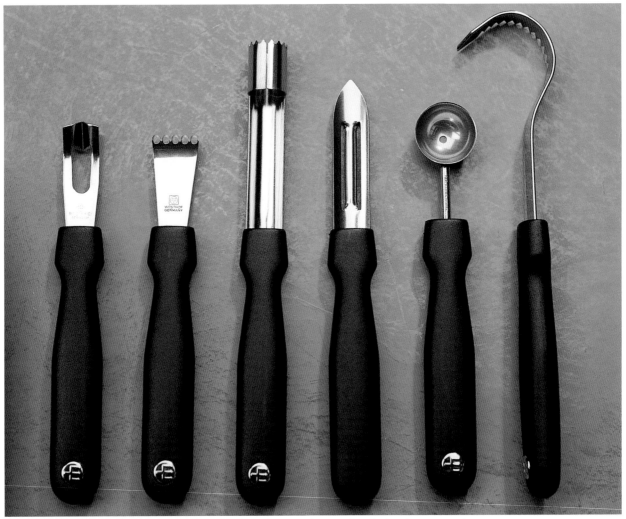

Pictured left to right: Channel knife, zester, corer, peeler, melon baler, butter curler

Specialty Garnishing Tools

These tools make easy work of a great number of kitchen chores. Here, I've highlighted their usefulness in creating garnishes.

• **Channel Knife:** Use it to carve strips in the skin of soft vegetables such as cucumbers and potatoes, as well as citrus fruits.

• **Zester:** When pulled against the peel of a piece of citrus fruit, it creates thin strips of zest. It can also be used to make vegetable shreds.

• **Corer:** This is used to remove the cores from fruits like apples and pears.

• **Peeler:** As its name indicates, this tool is used to peel vegetables and fruits. It can also be used to make very thin slices of vegetables or fruit. A swivel peeler (not shown here) is also excellent for vegetable peeling.

• **Melon Baller:** Not only does this make perfect little balls of melon, but it can also make balls of butter, cheese, potatoes or other soft items. It's also handy for scooping out cores and seeds of fruits and vegetables.

• **Butter Curler:** This is a one-function item, but it functions beautifully to make lovely curls of butter.

Graters

Graters come in a variety of shapes that have holes in a variety of sizes. The photo above shows flat handheld graters with hole sizes ranging from very fine to large. Handheld graters are perfect for a quick grate of lemon zest on a dessert or a little cheese on pasta. Thin handheld graters are called microplane rasps, and I am wild about them. They are very sharp and make quick work of grating.

Handy Tools to Keep On Hand

Skewers

Wooden or bamboo skewers are wonderful for little jobs like feathering sauces or positioning delicate items. They are inexpensive, and I consider them a kitchen essential.

Flexible Spatulas

Flexible spatulas – also known as scrapers – are a multi-use tool a cook can't do without. I have a whole drawer full of them. Ones made of silicone, which can withstand high heat, are great for stirring sauces.

Pastry Brushes

Use these to brush sauce on food and glazes on desserts or for greasing cake pans. I use my brushes most often for applying a thin coat of olive oil on bread when making bruschetta. Select brushes made with natural bristles rather than synthetic fibers; synthetic bristles don't absorb liquid as well as natural ones.

Utility Fork

A fork with two or three long, thin tines is useful for cooking, dipping items in chocolate, or skewering olives and pickles from jars.

Strainers & Sieves

Large and small strainers are handy for straining sauces. For garnishing, use them to sift sugar when frosting fruit and flowers, or to apply a dusting of powdered sugar or cocoa to desserts. Have at least two of them on hand: one for liquids, which can be washed and dried well, and another for dry items (sugar, flour, cocoa, etc.), which needn't be washed, just tapped and brushed with a dry towel.

Ricer

This tool makes a fine, airy mash of soft items such as hard boiled eggs and cooked root vegetables or fruits.

Mandoline

A mandoline is a handy luxury, not a necessity. Good quality, professional ones are durable and expensive. Use a mandoline for accomplishing paper thin slices, julienne vegetables, waffle cuts, crinkle cuts, matchstick pieces, and French fry cuts. Mandolines have changeable blades and can be adjusted for the thickness of the slice. The fruits and vegetables are moved across the blade with the use of a safety guard or pusher that protects your fingers from the blade, which is (trust me on this) **very** sharp.

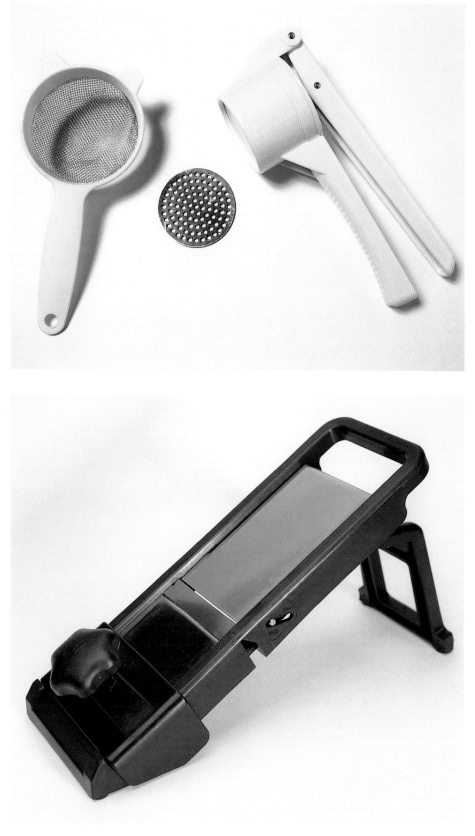

Choppers

Inexpensive choppers can be found in seemingly infinite variety. Most have a reservoir in which food is placed. The blades are plunged into the reservoir to cut and chop the food. I use mine most often for chopping nuts.

Plastic Squeeze Bottles

Besides being convenient containers for mustard and cat-sup, plastic squeeze bottles are a wonderful professional secret. Use them to make creative squirts and swirls of sauces, oils, and syrups on foods and serving dishes.

Garnishing Tools

Palette Knives

These flexible metal spatulas are most often used for spreading melted chocolate or icings on desserts, but they also are useful for spreading and smoothing sauces and butter. You'll want them in several sizes.

Canape Cutters

These can be used to cut almost anything into a decorative shape – sliced fruits and vegetables, pastry, bread slices, cheese, biscuits, and cookies.

Pastry Bag & Decorating Tips

The piping of icings and whipped toppings is easy to accomplish with a sturdy pastry bag and large-holed tip. They also can be used to fill pasta and pastry. The tips come in a variety of sizes and types that make different decorative shapes.

Parchment

Parchment can be used to make funnels and pastry bags, and it makes a wonderful non-stick liner for baking sheets or counter tops. It comes in rolls like wax paper and foil, both bleached (white) and unbleached (a beige color like that of brown paper bags).

3

Herbs & Spices

The splendid colors, textures, shapes, and flavors of fresh herbs make them the perfect (and probably most widely used) garnish for almost any dish – even dessert! A sprinkle of chopped herbs brightens up most any meat, fish, or soup. A single herb sprig, tucked under vegetables in a plate or bowl or inserted in a casserole, is an easy way to add just the right visual accent. The long, slender shape of chives can add a graceful, exotic touch when laid across a dish. I also like to tie bundles of cooked vegetables with long strands of chives or green onion or scallion tops. The possibilities are endless.

Use only fresh – never dried – herbs for garnishes. Dried herbs have unappealing textures and tastes if they haven't been reconstituted with liquid.

Common herbs to use as garnishes:
- Basil
- Bay leaves (fresh, not dried)
- Chives
- Dill
- Fennel
- Lemon verbena
- Marjoram
- Mint
- Parsley
- Rosemary
- Sage
- Sorrel
- Tarragon
- Thyme
- Oregano

Pictured opposite page, left to right: Top Row - Dill, sage, basil; Middle Row - Rosemary, chives, fresh bay leaves; Bottom Row - Flat leaf parsley, tarragon.

Chopped Herbs

To prepare herbs for chopping, wash them under running water, then roll the wet herbs between paper towels or spin them in a salad spinner to dry them.

Here's How:

1. **With a knife:** Place herbs on cutting board and chop them in one direction with a sharp chef's knife.

2. **For fine pieces:** Turn the cutting board to chop in the other direction to create fine pieces.

3. **With scissors:** You can also use scissors to cut small pieces of herbs. Chives are especially nice when cut with scissors.

Pictured main dish: A plate of meatloaf and mashed potatoes becomes a festive dinner with a sprinkling of snipped chives that decorates the plate like confetti. Long chive stems are laid across the mashed potatoes for a finishing touch.

Pictured breakfast dish: Eggs Baked in Brioche – sprinkled with snipped chives and placed on a plate that is garnished with a fanned strawberry (see the "Fruit" chapter) and some blueberries.

─ *recipe* ─

Eggs Baked in Brioche

Preheat the oven to 350 degrees F. Start with an individual size French brioche. Cut off the top third. Carefully scoop out the bottom piece, leaving the crust intact to make a bread bowl. Brush melted butter on the surface of the scooped-out bowl and on the cut side of the top. Arrange the brioche pieces on a baking sheet. Break one or two eggs into the bottom section (depending upon size of brioche). Bake both the bottoms and tops until eggs are cooked, 10 to 20 minutes. Remove from oven. Season eggs with salt and pepper, add garnish.

─ *recipe* ─

Chiffonade

A chiffonade is composed of fine slices of an herb. The slender strands of a chiffonade of herbs add color, flavor, and texture. The cutting technique works well with wide-leafed herbs and lettuces such as basil, mint, lemon verbena, or spinach.

Here's How:

1. **Stack** clean and dry leaves on top of one another, about 5 or 6 at a time.

2. **Roll up** the leaves lengthwise to make a tube.

3. **Shred finely**, cutting crosswise with a chef's knife.

Pictured appetizer: Tomato and fresh mozzarella bruschetta, garnished with a chiffonade of basil and a sprig of basil leaves.

---
recipe

Tomato & Mozzarella Bruschetta

Toast or grill slices of French or Italian bread. Place slices on a plate. Rub a cut clove of garlic on one side of the toasted surface of each bread slice. Brush the bread with olive oil or olive oil infused with basil. Top with a slice of tomato, then a slice of fresh mozzarella. Drizzle with some basil oil (see the "Sauces" chapter).

recipe

Fried Sage Leaves

Fried herbs give crisp little bursts of flavor to foods. Sage is the best herb to fry because of the thickness of the leaves. Fried sage leaves are great for garnishing creamy pasta dishes, eggs, potatoes, and creamy soups. They will keep for 3 to 4 days in a sealed container in the refrigerator.

Here's How:

1. **Wash** sage leaves and drain on a paper towel to remove excess water. Allow leaves to be damp.

Pictured main dish: A bowl of ravioli, sprinkled with grated cheese, is enlivened with lemon zest, fried sage leaves, and coarsely ground black pepper.

2. **Dust** each leaf with flour. Shake to remove excess flour.

3. **Fry.** Pour an inch of oil in a pan and heat to 365 degrees. Drop floured leaves (5 or 6 at a time) into hot oil for about 5 seconds – don't allow them to brown. Remove and drain on paper towels. Sprinkle lightly with salt.

Herb-Topped Breads

Biscuits and rolls look like pieces of art when you bake them with sprigs of herbs on top. You can add herbs to rolls (heat-and-serve, frozen, home-baked) or biscuits (prepared or homemade biscuit dough or frozen bake-and-serve). Use flat-leafed herbs such as parsley, cilantro, or dill.

Here's How:

1. **Brush.** Beat an egg white with 1 tablespoon of water until it just begins to foam. Brush this mixture on top of the roll or biscuit.

2. **Decorate.** While still moist, place one or more herb sprigs on top. Use one herb or a variety.

Pictured: These frozen biscuits will fool any guest into believing that they are made from scratch. Dill and parsley decorate the tops.

3. **Brush again.** Carefully brush more of the egg white mixture over the herbs to flatten them. Bake as directed in the roll or biscuit recipe.

26

Herb-Topped Pastry

Herbs look quite lovely on savory pastries, and they add wonderful flavor to the dish. Any type of main dish casserole would look wonderful topped with an herb crust, and the addition of an herb-topped pastry makes a wonderful presentation for most any meat, fish, or vegetable dish. You can buy prepared pie dough or make your own.

Pictured main dish: This crust – decorated with parsley, dill, and sage leaves – covers a savory chicken pie.

Here's How:

1. **Roll.** Roll out the pie dough. When it is flat and nearly to size, place herbs of your choice on the dough. Use the rolling pin to continue to roll out the dough to the correct size, pressing the herbs into the dough.

2. **Brush and bake.** Beat an egg white with 1 tablespoon of water until it just begins to foam. Carefully brush this mixture on top of the dough using a pastry brush. Place the crust on the pie or casserole and bake according to your recipe.

Sprinklings of Spices

Like gold dust, a sprinkling of a spice can add just the right sparkle and pizzazz to a dish. Because the flavors of spices are more intense than those of herbs they must be used more sparingly.

Guidelines for Using Spices

Pepper – There are a dozen varieties of peppercorns in various colors for adding zing and color to foods. Mix several colors of peppercorns in your pepper mill for the prettiest garnish. A grind or two atop creamy soups makes the soup all the more tempting. Dress the edges of meat plates with ground pepper. Always use fresh ground pepper for the best flavor. The ground pepper you buy in a can or jar doesn't have the flavor of fresh-ground – it adds bitterness (and just a little heat) to foods.

Coarse Sea Salt – Sea salt is much more intense than the iodized table variety, and the taste is a world apart. Look for salt without additives, and experiment with different types of salt to find ones that suit you. (They all taste salty, of course, but there are subtle differences.) You can also grind your own salt for even more intense flavor. Sprinkle a bit on sliced tomatoes for a beautiful presentation.

Paprika – This old standby is most often seen on country potato salad and deviled eggs at potluck dinners. Paprika, like most powdered spices, can lose its flavor quickly, so buy a fresh supply every two months. Smoked paprika has a wonderful flavor and color; sprinkle it on omelets, deviled eggs, and light-colored creamy vegetable soups. Hot paprika is also available to add a kick to your food.

Cayenne Pepper – Be very judicious with this ground red pepper – it packs a punch. Creamy dishes such as asparagus custard or shrimp-and-cream cheese spread look and taste great with a cayenne sprinkle.

Chili Pepper Powder – Buy pure ground chili pepper, not a blended chili

powder that contains garlic and other additives. Many southwestern food purveyors sell brilliant red chili pepper powder made from Santa Fe chilies. There is also a very flavorful green chili variety. These are *picante* – spicy hot – so be careful. Sprinkle chili pepper on southwestern or Mexican foods, especially light-colored foods such as guacamole or cream soups, or on top of the sour cream that garnishes a quesadilla or frijoles. To garnish darker-colored foods, sprinkle on the edge of the plate.

Curry Powders – Curry powders lend flavor and color to deviled eggs, omelets, and cream soups. They are blends of several spices and can be mild, savory, spicy, or hot. To some, curry powder is an acquired taste. I use curry powder to flavor a favorite appetizer spread – I mix some chutney with cream cheese, mound it in a beautiful dish, and sprinkle with curry powder. Serve with sesame crackers or pita bread triangles.

Ginger – Ginger's spicy sweetness complements vegetables and fruits. Sprinkle ground ginger on a bowl of cream of carrot soup. Slice a mango and other tropical fruit on a plate, then dust the plate edge with ginger. Sprinkle it on a blueberry smoothie.

Cinnamon – Even a raw sliced apple becomes more appealing with a sprinkle of cinnamon. In the fall and winter I like to make a cooked apple compote to top off pancakes or waffles on Sunday morning. A sprinkle of cinnamon completes the dish. When I make an apple pie, I sprinkle the top crust with sugar and cinnamon before baking.

Nutmeg – Buy whole nutmeg and grate on a microplane rasp – the taste will amaze you! Sprinkle grated nutmeg on a creamy chicken dish or casserole. Butternut squash soup with a sprinkle of grated nutmeg tastes like golden autumn. A very light dusting is great on cappuccino.

— recipe —

Blue Cheese Stuffed Dates

A sprinkle of cayenne pepper adds a punch of flavor at the end of each bite. These stuffed dates, with their combination of sweet and hot, make a delightful before-dinner snack. This mixture will fill about 16 dates.

1. Mix 4 oz. cream cheese with 4 oz. of crumbled blue cheese.
2. Split dates and remove seeds. Spread dates open.
3. Fill each date with about 1 Tbsp. of cheese mix. Press date slightly to close.
4. Place an almond or almond sliver on top of each one.
5. Dust dates and plate with cayenne pepper.

— recipe —

Pictured appetizer or dessert: Blue cheese stuffed dates are topped with Spanish blanched almonds and sprinkled with cayenne pepper. Stuff dates by piping cream cheese for a prettier presentation. See Chapter 7 for piping how to. You can garnish the plate (as I did) with additional almonds. Serve with wine or sherry.

Herb & Cheese Spreads

Keep some cream cheese and goat cheese in your refrigerator to combine with fresh herbs or powdered spices for colorful instant appetizers. It couldn't be easier, tastier, or prettier. Just shape the cheese into balls or logs, then coat with chopped herbs or powdered spices. Following are other recipes for quick and easy spreads for crackers.

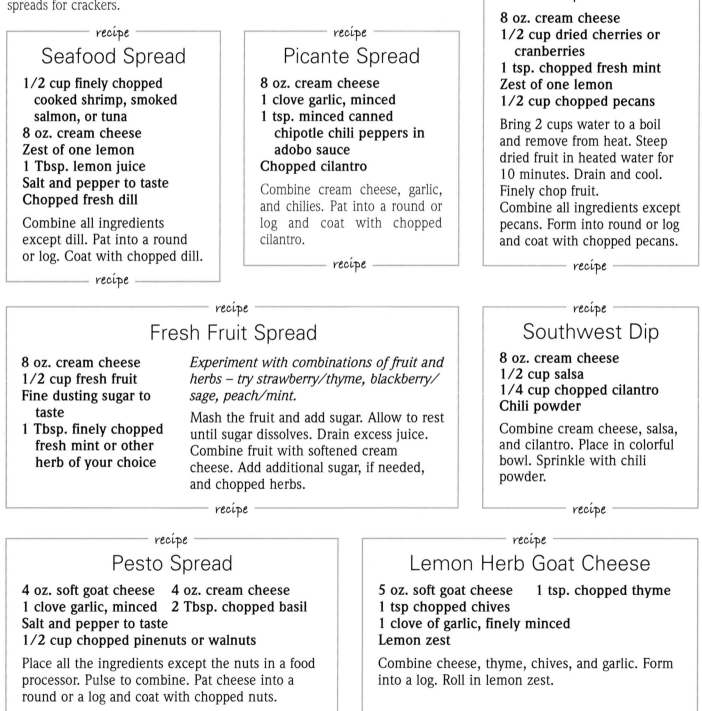

recipe

Seafood Spread

1/2 cup finely chopped cooked shrimp, smoked salmon, or tuna
8 oz. cream cheese
Zest of one lemon
1 Tbsp. lemon juice
Salt and pepper to taste
Chopped fresh dill

Combine all ingredients except dill. Pat into a round or log. Coat with chopped dill.

recipe

Picante Spread

8 oz. cream cheese
1 clove garlic, minced
1 tsp. minced canned chipotle chili peppers in adobo sauce
Chopped cilantro

Combine cream cheese, garlic, and chilies. Pat into a round or log and coat with chopped cilantro.

recipe

Minty Dried Fruit Spread

8 oz. cream cheese
1/2 cup dried cherries or cranberries
1 tsp. chopped fresh mint
Zest of one lemon
1/2 cup chopped pecans

Bring 2 cups water to a boil and remove from heat. Steep dried fruit in heated water for 10 minutes. Drain and cool. Finely chop fruit.
Combine all ingredients except pecans. Form into round or log and coat with chopped pecans.

recipe

Fresh Fruit Spread

8 oz. cream cheese
1/2 cup fresh fruit
Fine dusting sugar to taste
1 Tbsp. finely chopped fresh mint or other herb of your choice

Experiment with combinations of fruit and herbs – try strawberry/thyme, blackberry/sage, peach/mint.

Mash the fruit and add sugar. Allow to rest until sugar dissolves. Drain excess juice. Combine fruit with softened cream cheese. Add additional sugar, if needed, and chopped herbs.

recipe

Southwest Dip

8 oz. cream cheese
1/2 cup salsa
1/4 cup chopped cilantro
Chili powder

Combine cream cheese, salsa, and cilantro. Place in colorful bowl. Sprinkle with chili powder.

recipe

Pesto Spread

4 oz. soft goat cheese   4 oz. cream cheese
1 clove garlic, minced   2 Tbsp. chopped basil
Salt and pepper to taste
1/2 cup chopped pinenuts or walnuts

Place all the ingredients except the nuts in a food processor. Pulse to combine. Pat cheese into a round or a log and coat with chopped nuts.

recipe

Lemon Herb Goat Cheese

5 oz. soft goat cheese   1 tsp. chopped thyme
1 tsp chopped chives
1 clove of garlic, finely minced
Lemon zest

Combine cheese, thyme, chives, and garlic. Form into a log. Roll in lemon zest.

recipe

Pictured appetizers, clockwise from top left: Balls of cream cheese rolled in ground peppercorns, lavender seeds, chili powder, lemon zest, and snipped chives; herb crackers (pie dough cut in cracker shapes using canape cutters and topped with herbs – see page 27 for details); goat cheese log coated with a variety of chopped herbs.

Rosemary Skewers

Long, sturdy branches of rosemary make wonderful skewers for grilled shrimp, scallops, or grilled vegetable kabobs. They provide a pretty presentation and impart a hint of flavor. Since shrimp or scallops don't take long to cook, the skewers don't get burned.

Here's How:

1. **Select** sturdy branches of rosemary and soak in water until ready to use.

2. **Peel** fresh shrimp, leaving the tails intact and de-vein by making a slit down back and pulling out black vein.

3. **Thread** shrimp on skewers from the bottom (cut) ends of the branches.

---

recipe

Grilled Rosemary Shrimp

Serve with remoulade sauce or your favorite dipping sauce.

Raw shrimp, 6 per person
Rosemary branches, 1 for every 3 shrimp
1/4 cup olive oil
Grated zest of 1 lemon
Juice of one lemon
Salt & Pepper

1. Combine olive oil, lemon juice, and lemon zest. Place peeled and de-veined shrimp in olive oil mixture. Let marinate for 15 minutes.
2. Thread 3 shrimp on each skewer.
3. Heat grill on high. Place skewers on grill and cook about 2 minutes per side or until shrimp are pink.

recipe

32

4
Vegetable Garnishes

Fresh vegetables are so versatile – they can be sliced, julienned, grated, curled, cut with small cookie cutters, left whole, and even carved. Carrots, squash, peppers, tomatoes, radishes, broccoli, cauliflower, beets, cucumbers, green onions, potatoes, turnips – these are just a few from a long list of raw vegetables to use as garnishes.

And don't forget cooked vegetables. Shred and deep fry them for crispy color. Carve cooked potatoes into mushroom shapes. Or cut carrots or winter squash or turnips into shapes and cook them.

Vegetable Confetti

Diced vegetable confetti adds a shower of color to a plate. Vegetables that work well for this technique are ones that hold a shape, like carrots, bell peppers, cucumbers, and celery. If using cucumbers, leave unpeeled and use only strips cut from the outside without seeds.

Here's How:

1. **Slice** the vegetables (here, it's celery) into long, thin strips.

2. **Chop.** Arrange several strips to make an even bundle. Using a chef's knife, cut the strips crosswise into tiny dice.

Pictured appetizer: These eggrolls make a festive appetizer when garnished with a colorful confetti of chopped red, yellow, and orange bell peppers and chopped cucumbers. Orange ginger dipping sauce, served in a tiny dish, is the perfect accompaniment. Using frozen eggrolls makes this an easy appetizer to prepare.

Julienne Garnishes

Thin matchsticks of colorful vegetables make a quick, lovely garnish. Choose sturdy vegetables that can be cut into long strips, such as celery, ginger root, bell pepper, or carrots and other root vegetables such as parsnips and turnips.

Here's How:

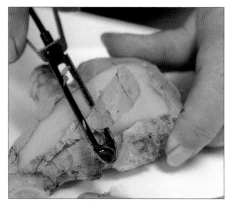  

1. **Peel** the vegetable, if needed for better flavor or appearance. I'm peeling this piece of ginger root with a swivel peeler to remove the tough brown skin.

2. **Slice and stack.** Slice the vegetable into strips or rings, depending upon the vegetable's shape. Stack the slices.

3. **Slice again,** using a chef's knife to create thin matchsticks.

Vegetable Bundles

A bundle of julienne vegetable pieces is a pretty way to garnish a bowl of soup. I use green onion tops or chives to wrap the bundles.

To prepare green onion tops, wash carefully, place in a dish, and pour boiling water over them. They will soften quickly in the hot water – don't leave them too long or they will lose color. Plunge them into ice water, then drain and cool.

If you're using chives, they are thin enough to tie around the bundle without the use of hot water.

Here's How:

1. **Peel, then slice.** Peel the vegetable if needed or desired for better flavor or appearance, then cut the vegetable into thin slices.

2. **Stack, then slice again.** Stack the slices, then cut into fine matchstick pieces, using a chef's knife.

3. **Cut** the prepared green onion top into narrow strips.

4. **Wrap** the center of a bundle of julienne carrot sticks with a strip of the green onion. Knot to secure.

Pictured soup course: This vibrantly colored carrot soup is garnished with swirls of creme fraiche feathered with a skewer. A bundle of julienne fresh ginger root tied with a green onion top finishes the dish.

37

Spinach Frizzles

Colorful strands of crisp fried spinach are a great garnish for light-colored foods. Use spinach frizzles to garnish pasta, rice, potatoes, meats, or casseroles. Here mushroom ravioli with Alfredo sauce makes a hearty main dish. Grated Parmesan cheese was sprinkled on the ravioli and the edge of the plate before the spinach frizzles were placed.

To Prepare the Leaves

1. **Wash, dry, stack.** Wash and dry the spinach thoroughly. Stack the leaves on a cutting board.

2. **Roll** the leaves to make a tube.

3. **Slice.** Thinly slice into a fine chiffonade using a chef's knife or slicing knife.

---
recipe

Fried Spinach

1. **Heat** 2 inches of vegetable oil in a deep skillet to 375 degrees F.
2. **Cook.** Drop a handful of spinach chiffonade into the oil. Cook only until the oil no longer sputters and the spinach is deep green, about 3 seconds. Remove spinach immediately, using a mesh skimmer or slotted spoon.
3. **Drain** on paper towels. Cook spinach in small batches. Bring the oil back to the correct temperature for each batch to ensure that the spinach is crisp.

recipe

Fried Vegetable Shreds

Fried vegetable shreds make a crispy garnish for meats. Starchy vegetables such as white potatoes, sweet potatoes, and carrots work well for this technique. Here a nest of fried potato shreds garnishes a grilled steak. Steamed asparagus tied with a green onion strip completes the meal.

To Prepare the Shreds

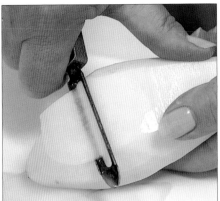

1. **Cut** a peeled potato into very thin slices. (A vegetable peeler can be used to make the slices, as shown here.)

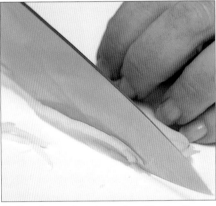

2. **Stack and cut again.** Stack slices and cut into a fine julienne.

3. **Soak.** Put the shreds in ice water. Use tongs to separate the shreds while they are in the ice water.

---
recipe

Fried Potatoes

1. **Prepare.** Heat oil to 375 degrees F. While the oil heats, drain the vegetable shreds and pat completely dry between several layers of paper towels.
2. **Fry** in small batches until golden and crisp, 1 to 1-1/2 minutes per batch, gently separating and stirring once or twice while frying.
3. **Drain.** Transfer to paper towels to drain, using a mesh skimmer or slotted spoon. Season with salt and pepper. Be sure the oil comes back to the correct temperature before adding the next batch.

Hot Pepper Flowers

Flowers made from hot chili peppers are great for garnishing food with a southwestern flair – the pepper garnish signals your guests that the food has heat. Choose long, narrow peppers with thin flesh for best results.

Remember to handle the peppers carefully, to avoid touching your eyes as you work, and to wash your hands thoroughly when you're finished. (Wear gloves if your hands are sensitive.)

Here's How:

1. **Cut.** Using scissors, snip into the pepper from the tip, making small, triangle-shaped cuts. Cut as close to the base of the pepper as you can. Remove the seeds with the point of the knife or scrape out with a skewer.

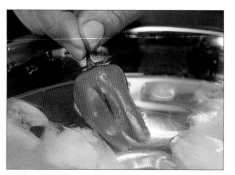

2. **Soak.** Place the cut pepper in a bowl of ice water. It will curl. Store the peppers in a bowl of ice water in the refrigerator until you're ready to use them. Drain on a towel before placing on food.

Radish Roses

Choose round red radishes for roses. They are great for garnishing cold meat or vegetable salads as well as cold sandwiches. A pairing knife is best for this technique.

Here's How:

1. **Cut the end.** Cut the root tip from the radish, exposing a small circle of white.

2. **Cut the first petal.** Cut a petal of skin on the side of the radish, leaving it attached at the base.

3. **Cut more petals.** Cut 3 or 4 more petals, spacing them evenly around the radish.

4. **Soak.** Place in a bowl of ice water – they will open. Drain before using.

40

Curly Green Onions

This technique works just as well with the green stalk of the onion as it does with the white bulb. In the photos, the bulb part of the onion is shaped into a curly brush.

Here's How:

1. **Prepare.** Wash the green onion carefully and trim off some of the green top, leaving about 2 to 3 inches of green. Trim the root from the bulb.

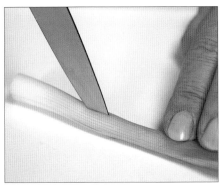

2. **Cut.** Make thin cuts through the white bulb of onion.

3. **Soak.** Place the cut end in ice water and watch it curl. Drain before using as a garnish.

Pictured soup course or main dish: A curly green onion garnishes a bowl of black bean soup. A dish of sour cream that can be mixed into the soup is garnished with a hot pepper flower.

Cucumbers

The soft flesh of cucumbers is easy to cut and shape into attractive garnishes. For best results, purchase European-style cucumbers – they have fewer seeds and thinner skins, and look for cucumbers that have not been waxed. Do not peel cucumbers you are using for garnish. Here are a few ways they can be made into garnishes.

Slices

Make your slices more attractive by cutting grooves in the skin.

1. **Make grooves** along the length of the cucumber, using a channel knife.

2. **Slice** the cucumber into thin slices.

Fans

Cucumber fans make great borders on salad plates or meat or seafood platters.

1. **Cut** the cucumber in half lengthwise, or leave whole. Place on a cutting board, cut side down. Make very thin crosswise slices, making sure not to cut all the way through the skin. Make 6 to 8 slices, then cut off the slices from the rest of the cucumber.

2. **Fan.** Use your fingers to push down on the uncut side and fan out the slices.

Shreds

Colorful shreds of cucumber skin make a great garnish when placed atop a dollop of mayonnaise or sour cream.

1. **Pull** a citrus zester along the skin of the cucumber.

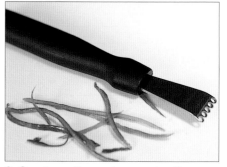

2. **See** how the zester creates fine shreds of bright green skin.

recipe

Dilled Tuna Salad Preparation

To create this dish, I first placed the tuna salad in a small rounded bowl and pressed it down with a rubber spatula. I overturned the bowl on a salad plate and lifted it away to reveal a neat mound of salad. I created a border with five cucumber fans placed evenly around the plate. Between the fans, I tucked dill sprigs and topped them with carrot curls and slices of green onion. The tuna mound is topped with sprigs of dill and a grooved cucumber slice.

To make carrot curls, use a vegetable peeler to slice off thin strips of carrot. Plunge the pieces into ice water to curl. Drain before using.

recipe

Candied Carrot Curls

Carrot curls are pretty, but candied carrot curls are divine. Use plain carrot curls to top sandwiches, and candied curls on desserts, ice cream, and meat dishes. Candied carrot curls are an especially appropriate garnish for a piece of carrot cake, as shown in the photo, *opposite.*

Here's How:

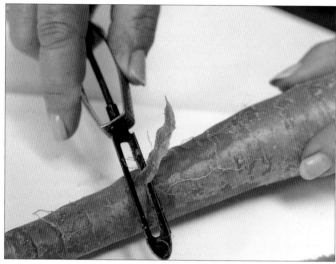

1. **Peel** a carrot with a vegetable peeler.

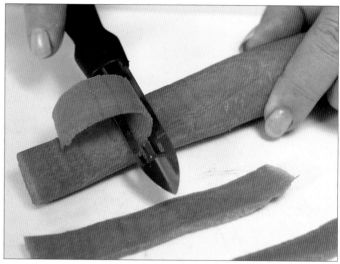

2. **Slice and dry.** Using a mandoline or vegetable peeler, cut thin strips of carrot. Dry the carrot strips between paper towels.

3. **Cook.** Put 2 cups water and 2 cups sugar in a saucepan and bring to a boil. Reduce the heat to medium and add the carrot strips. Cook until the carrots begin to turn translucent – 20 to 30 minutes. Remove carrot strips to a piece of parchment to cool enough to handle.

4. **Sugar.** Put some dusting granulated superfine sugar in a dish. Place the carrot strips in the dish to coat each curl. Remove strips to a clean piece of parchment and shape into curls. Allow to cool and harden. These can be stored in an air-tight container in the refrigerator for approximately one week.

44

Pickled Ginger Roses

Sushi lovers will be delighted with this beautiful presentation of pickled ginger. Purchase sliced (not shredded) pickled ginger root and drain the liquid from the package. Reserve the liquid for storing the remaining, unused ginger.

Pictured appetizer course: A ginger rose takes center stage on a plate of vegetable sushi. Cilantro sprigs mimic rose leaves. A dollop of wasabi cream finishes the plate.

Here's How:

1. **Roll** a slice of ginger to form a cylinder for the center of the rose.

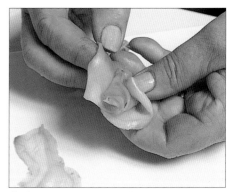

2. **Add the petals.** Use small pieces of sliced ginger for the petals, adding them one at a time and crimping them at the bottom. Roll the top edges back on some petals for a more natural look.

3. **Squeeze and place.** When you have added all the petals you desire, squeeze the base of the rose, place on the serving plate, and arrange the petals, if needed.

Tomato Roses

Tomato roses are easy to make and elegant to behold. All you need are a sharp paring knife and a medium-size round tomato. Here, I've used a red tomato, but a yellow one would also be lovely.

Here's How:

1. **Peel.** Starting at the bottom of the tomato, cut away the peel in a long ribbon. Try not to cut too much of the flesh so the slice will be thin enough to roll. Don't worry if you can't cut one continuous ribbon – pieces will work fine.

2. **Roll.** When the entire tomato is peeled, start rolling the strip with the end from the tomato top, shiny side out. Roll tightly at the base.

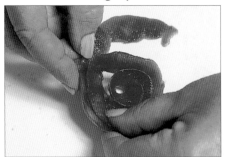

3. **Tuck.** When you reach the end, tuck the end of the tomato strip under the rose.

Pictured salad: Serve this Caprese salad as an individual salad course. A vivid red tomato rose sits in the center of five thin rounds of fresh mozzarella cheese. Basil sprigs, placed around the rose, look like leaves. Basil oil garnishes slices of mozzarella. See Chapter 6 for basil oil how to. Dots of a balsamic vinegar reduction squeezed from a plastic bottle are placed between the cheese slices. Sprinkle all with coarse sea salt. At the table, provide extra virgin olive oil for drizzling over the salad. Serve with crusty bread.

To make balsamic reduction: Simply boil a bottle of balsamic vinegar until reduced to a syrup. I sometimes use a product called Saba to garnish with instead of balsamic reduction. It is a syrup used to make balsamic vinegar. It has a sweet, tart, and malty taste that is great on salads and appetizers.

Garnishes for Soups

Soup can be an appetizer, a side dish, the main course, or a dessert. It can be savory or sweet, heavy or light – there's an almost endless variety of wonderful recipes to try. Soup is one of my favorite dishes to cook, garnish, and eat. Since so many soups are vegetable soups, I included them in this chapter.

---
recipe

Easy Gazpacho

Serves 4.

4 cups canned tomatoes *or* skinned and seeded fresh tomatoes
1 European cucumber
1 small/medium onion
1 red bell pepper
1 clove garlic
1/4 cup fresh cilantro or parsley
Juice of 1 lemon
1 Tbsp. olive oil
Optional: 1 jalapeño chili pepper
Salt and pepper to taste

1. Coarsely chop all vegetables and place them in a food processor. Add lemon and olive oil.
2. Process to the stage you like, from a chunky blend to a smooth puree. Taste and season with salt and pepper.

recipe

Guidelines for Garnishing Soup

Thick, hearty soups can take substantial garnishes, such as:

- Toasted bread slices topped with melted cheese or a smear of soft goat cheese

- Vegetable cutouts, raw or cooked

- Slices of tomato or cucumber sprinkled with herbs

- A dollop of sour cream

- Shredded cheese

- Citrus slices (on a hearty fish soup)

Creamed soups need lighter garnishes, such as:

- Sprinkles of fresh herbs or powdered spices

- Swirls or drizzles of pureed vegetables in a contrasting color

- Croutons

- Baked puff pastry shapes

- Very thin slices of vegetables

- Chiffonade of lettuce (on gazpacho or chili)

- Lemon zest

- Grated Parmesan cheese

- Coarsely ground pepper

Pictured opposite: Gazpacho with garnishes of chopped green onion, tomato, and cucumber.

5
Fruit Garnishes

Colorful fruits are popular, easy garnishes for salads, breakfast plates, desserts, and even meat dishes. Some fruit garnishes require little in the way of preparation – a luscious blueberry or raspberry placed on pudding is perfection, pure and simple.

A slice of kiwi adds a vivid green color and an interesting pattern. Blackberries have a jewel-like deep purple color and a great texture. Strawberries, another popular garnish, are great with chocolate, breakfast dishes, and even salads.

Lemons are a great addition to foods that need a tangy burst of flavor, such as fish. Because citrus fruits – oranges, lemons, and limes – are available year-round, think of them as the old stand-bys for adding color and bright, clean flavor.

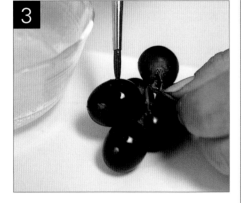

Frosted Grapes

This garnish is equally at home with desserts, salads, or meat plates. You can use one type of grapes or a variety of colors. Since the egg white isn't cooked, be sure to purchase pasteurized eggs or pasteurized egg whites.

Pictured main dish: Clusters of frosted red flame and green grapes garnish a roasted chicken. Fresh bay leaves, kumquats, and lady apples are placed between the clusters of grapes.

Here's How:
1. **Wash and snip.** Wash and dry grapes. Snip into small clusters, using kitchen scissors.
2. **Beat** an egg white with a wire whisk until slightly frothy.
3. **Paint.** Use a pastry brush or small paint brush to paint egg white on the grapes.
4. **Dust.** Place the painted grape cluster in a shallow bowl of fine granulated sugar. Dust cluster with more sugar. Shake off excess sugar. Place the clusters on parchment paper or a rack to dry. Use immediately.

Strawberry Fans

Here's How:

1. **Remove the hull.** Use a strawberry huller or a small knife to remove the green hull (the bracts and the stem end).

2. **Cut.** Hold the strawberry or place on a cutting board, stem side down. Make 5 or 6 thin cuts into the berry, coming as close to base as possible without cutting through.

3. **Make the fan.** Twist to fan out the slices. Place a mint sprig in the hole at the top of the berry where the hull used to be. (The mint sprig mimics the strawberry leaves.)

Pictured dessert: A special dessert calls for a special embellishment. Here, the top of a mini chocolate bundt cake is drizzled with chocolate fudge sauce and sprinkled with sliced almonds. Strawberry fans alternate with blackberries encircled with pieces of lemon zest to make a border. Drops of mint-infused whipping cream are placed around the blackberries.

Pear Fans

Firm, nearly ripe pears are poached in a simple sugar syrup and fashioned into fans. If you like, substitute white or red wine for some of the water in the poaching liquid. (With red wine, the pears will be deep pink.)

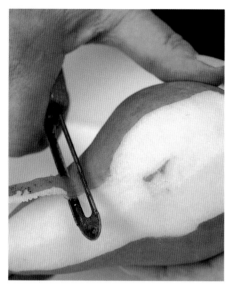

1. **Peel** pears and cut in half lengthwise. A swivel peeler is best for this.

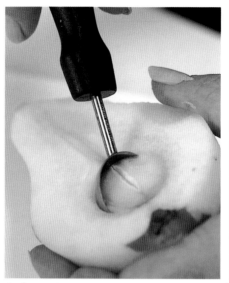

2. **Core.** Use a melon baller to scoop out the seeds.

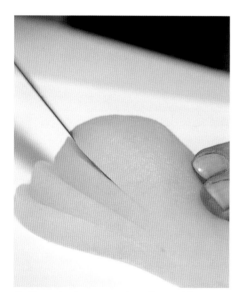

3. **Poach** the pears for about 10 minutes in a syrup of 2 cups liquid (water or water and wine) and 1 cup of sugar. Test pears with a skewer to make sure they are soft. Allow pears to cool in syrup.

4. **Slice.** Remove the pears from the syrup and slice into very thin slices, leaving the stem end intact. Place on the serving dish and press gently with your fingers.

recipe

Vanilla Cream Sauce

2 cups half and half cream
2 large eggs
1/2 cup sugar
1 vanilla bean, halved lengthwise *or* 1 tsp. vanilla extract

1. Place half and half in a heavy saucepan.
2. Using a paring knife, scrape the seeds from the vanilla bean. Add the seeds and the bean to the saucepan. Bring to a boil, then remove from heat.
3. Whisk together eggs and sugar in a bowl until combined.
4. Add the hot half and half mixture in a slow stream, whisking constantly.
5. Pour the mixture back in the saucepan and cook over low heat, stirring constantly with a wooden spoon, until thickened. **Do not** let boil. Chill in refrigerator, covered, until cold.

recipe

Pictured dessert opposite: This pear fan is more than a garnish – it's the best part of the dessert. It adorns a piece of spice cake. Underneath it all, there's a pool of vanilla cream sauce. A mint sprig is used as a garnish.

Sliced Citrus

Citrus rings, spirals, and funnels add a bright, refreshing note to foods. They're quick and easy to make.

Citrus Rings

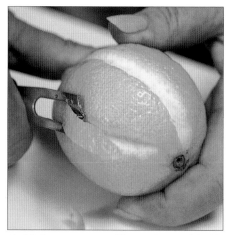

1. **Make grooves.** Use a channel knife to make vertical cuts all around the rind of the fruit. (The grooves make the ring look more interesting.)

2. **Slice** crosswise. Make thin slices for decorating a serving dish, thicker slices if you are garnishing a glass.

Citrus Funnels or Spirals

1. **Cut** the fruit in half. Cut thin slices from either side of the center. Make a slit from one edge to the center of the slice.

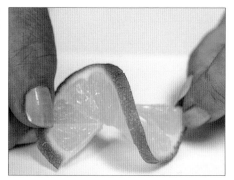

2. **For a spiral**, twist the slice and place ends on plate apart from one another.

3. **For a funnel**, overlap the cut sides.

Pictured appetizer: A margarita or martini glass makes a fun serving container for guacamole. Rub the rim of the glass with a lime slice, then dip in coarse salt. Fill with guacamole. Garnish the rim of the glass with a slice from a channel-cut lime. (See the "Sauces" chapter for the guacamole recipe.)

Pictured cocktail opposite: A lemon twist garnishes a cosmopolitan martini. To make the lemon twist, use a channel knife to pull a strip of peel. Twist the strip, then plunge it in ice water for a few minutes so it will hold this shape.

Citrus Zest

This is one of my very favorite garnishes. It is so easy, yet it adds much in the way of visual appeal and the bright citrus taste adds a spark of flavor to any dish.

---
recipe ———

Dilled Cream Cheese Spread

This will keep in the refrigerator for 3 days.

4 oz. cream cheese
1 Tbsp. sour cream
1 Tbsp. lemon juice
2 Tbsp. chopped dill
1 Tbsp. chopped capers
1 Tbsp. finely minced onion
Salt and pepper to taste

Combine all ingredients, using a fork or a food processor.

——— *recipe* ———

With a zester. Using a zester is the easiest way to get even, thin strips that curl beautifully. Simply pull the zester along the fruit. Shreds can be chopped with a chef's knife if a finer zest is desired.

Pictured opposite page: Whether it is an appetizer, a light lunch, or an afternoon snack, foods you serve should look as good as they taste. Here, thick slices of French bread are spread with dilled cream cheese and topped with thin slices of smoked salmon. Lemon zest and dill sprigs garnish the pieces.

With a grater. Rub the skin of the fruit across a fine grater or microplane rasp as shown here to make tiny shreds.

Candied Citrus Peel

Candied citrus peel makes an elegant garnish for a dessert. Julienne strips of citrus peel are cooked in a sugar syrup and dusted with granulated sugar. The peels of oranges, lemons, limes, and grapefruits can be used. Here, I've used an orange.

Candied peel can be kept several weeks in a sealed container. Store in a dry place.

Here's How:

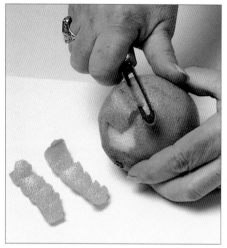

1. **Peel.** With a vegetable peeler, remove large strips of peel from the citrus fruit.

2. **Stack and slice.** Stack the strips of peel and julienne with a chef's knife.

3. **Cook.** In a heavy saucepan, place 1 cup sugar and 1 cup water. Bring to a boil, stirring constantly to dissolve the sugar. Place the peel in the syrup and boil until peel becomes translucent, 15 to 20 minutes.

4. **Remove** the peel with tongs or a slotted spoon and place in bowl of fine sugar. Toss the peel in the sugar to coat.

5. **Let dry.** Place on a sheet of parchment or a rack to dry and harden.

Pictured dessert opposite: A chocolate pot au creme is topped with a dollop of whipped cream and crowned with candied citrus peel. A mint sprig adds some color to the plate.

Candied Citrus Slices

You can also make candied citrus slices to use as a garnish. Here, I've used lemon slices. I saved the lemony syrup, let it cool in the refrigerator, and used it to flavor and sauce a dessert of Lemon Cream Crepes.

Here's How:

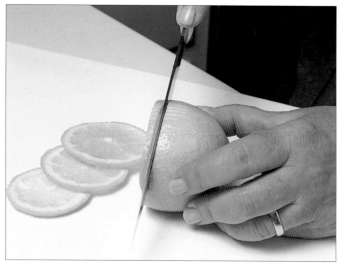

1. **Slice and blanch.** Slice 1 or 2 lemons into very thin slices using a knife or mandoline. Remove the seeds. Blanch slices in boiling water for 1 minute. Place in ice water for 1 minute to cool. Drain.

2. **Cook.** In a heavy pan, dissolve 1 cup sugar in 1 cup water and bring to a boil. Place slices in syrup and cook until slices are translucent, 30 to 45 minutes.

3. **Remove** slices and place on a piece of parchment to dry.

---
recipe
Lemon Cream Crepes

Serves 4.

8 crepes (purchased or homemade)
4 oz. cream cheese
1 cup whipping cream
Cooled lemony syrup from candied citrus slices
8 to 12 candied citrus slices

1. Using an electric mixer or whisk, beat cream cheese with 2 Tbsp. whipping cream until softened.
2. In another bowl, use the mixer or whisk to beat the remaining cream with 2 Tbsp. lemony syrup until stiff.
3. Fold the cream cheese into the lemony cream.
4. Place a dollop of the cream mixture on the center of each crepe. Fold the crepe into fourths. Repeat, filling and folding all the crepes.
5. Stack 2 crepes on each plate. Drizzle with some of the lemony syrup. Garnish with candied citrus slices.

recipe

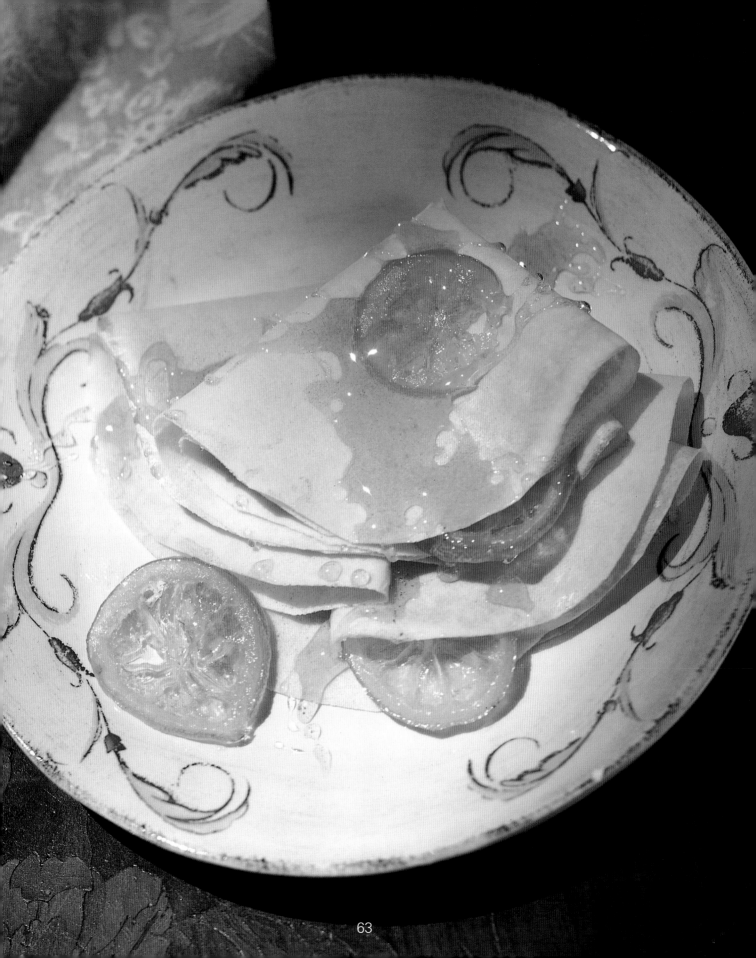

Citrus Bowls

Citrus fruit rinds make convenient little bowls for desserts, sauces, and dips. The best part is not having to wash them when you're finished – just toss them. (You can always make more.) Citrus bowls can be held in the refrigerator for an hour or so until you're ready to use them. Save the flesh for fruit salad.

Pictured above: Use a lime cup as a container for guacamole. (See the "Sauces" chapter for the guacamole recipe.)

Pictured dessert, opposite page: Here is the perfect summer treat – fruit sorbet served in citrus bowls. Place the softened sorbet in the citrus bowls and chill in the freezer an hour or more before serving. Mint sprigs garnish the sorbet cups.

Here's How:

1. **Cut.** Cut fruit in half. With a grapefruit spoon or a small, sharp paring knife, cut around the perimeter of fruit next to the white part of the rind, keeping the rind intact.

2. **Remove flesh.** Use a grapefruit spoon to remove fruit sections and scrape the fibrous membrane from the inside of the rind. Save fruit sections for another recipe.

64

Mango Squares

Little squares of mango can be used to accent a dish or as part of a fruit cup or salad. This easy cutting trick – removing the fruit in sections from around the flattened oval pit – results in perfect, juicy squares.

Here's How:

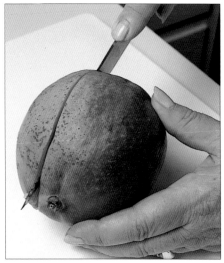

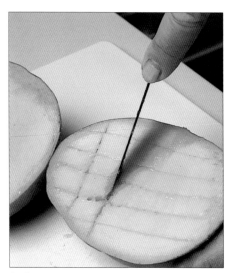

1. **Cut.** Wash the mango. Without peeling, slice the fleshy part off each side of the fruit, coming as close to the pit as possible. Cut off the flesh from the sides around the pit.

2. **Score** the flesh in a crosshatch pattern. (Half-inch cuts make a nice size for garnishing or salads.) Avoid cutting through the skin.

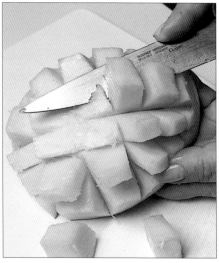

3. **Push** the skin side of piece to reverse the curve and reveal the cuts.

4. **Trim** off the mango cubes close to the skin.

Pictured salad above: This vibrantly colored Avocado Mango Salad is garnished with a lime wedge, mint leaves, and an edible orchid. See the "Edible Flowers" chapter for guidelines about using orchids.

Avocado Mango Salad

Serves 4 as a lunch entree.

For the salad:
2 mangoes, cut in 1/2" cubes
2 avocados, cut in 1/2" cubes
1/4 cup chopped red bell pepper
1 minced jalapeño chili pepper
8 mint leaves, cut in a chiffonade
1 Tbsp. snipped chives
Either: 1 cup of cooked chicken,
   or 1 cup cooked shrimp, *or*

3/4 cup mild cheese (such as
mozzarella or feta), cut in
1/2" cubes

For the dressing:
Juice of 1 lime
Juice of 1/2 orange
1/4 cup of olive oil
Salt and pepper to taste

Mix dressing ingredients with a
whisk. Pour over salad ingredients
and toss gently. Season with salt
and pepper to taste.

Melon Balls

Melon balls are one of the easiest garnishes to make. Use them on puddings, cold fruit soups, and fruit salads. The melon baller tool for making melon balls comes in several sizes – the choice is yours.

Here's How:

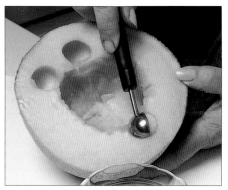

Simply push the tool into the flesh of the melon and rotate, then pull out the ball. Be sure to push the tool into the fruit so you will get a full, round ball, not a half-ball.

Pictured above: Cantaloupe soup is garnished with cantaloupe balls and tiny leaves of lemon verbena.

Pictured dessert, opposite page: Honeydew Mint Fool, garnished with honeydew balls and tiny pieces of lime zest, is presented in a stemmed martini glass centered on a green plate.

---
recipe

Honeydew Mint Fool

This is a light summery dessert. Mash, rather than puree, the honeydew cubes for a more interesting texture. Pureeing the fruit makes it watery and less flavorful.

Serves 4

1 cup heavy whipping cream
6 Tbsp. sugar
1 cup honeydew melon
   cubes
1 Tbsp. lime juice
1 Tbsp. chopped mint

1. Mash honeydew cubes.
2. Add 3 tbsp. sugar and lime juice to the mashed melon.
3. Beat the cream with 3 tbsp. sugar until stiff.
4. Fold in mashed fruit and chopped mint.

recipe

Fruit Glaze

A glossy glaze makes fresh fruit look even more luscious and colorful. At the same time, it preserves the fruit and keeps it fresh looking for hours.

Glazing is easy when you use jam or jelly. For a dark, rich-looking glaze, I like to use currant jelly. For a lighter colored glaze, I use apricot jam or apple jelly. Apply the glaze with a pastry brush to fruit tarts, custards, pastries, cakes, or breads. You can store leftover glaze in the refrigerator for up to one month. It can be re-melted and used.

Here's How:

1. **Melt.** Spoon 1 cup of jelly or jam into a saucepan. Add a squeeze of lemon juice and 1 tablespoon brandy. (If you have neither lemon juice nor brandy, substitute 1 tablespoon water.) Heat, stirring continually, until the jam is smooth and liquid. Simmer about 5 minutes.

2. **Brush** the melted jelly or jam on the area you wish to glaze, using a pastry brush. Allow to set up before serving.

Pictured dessert above: Vanilla cream tart covered with blackberries, strawberries, and blueberries. Glazing the fruit makes them gleam like jewels.

Pictured dessert, opposite page: A lemon chiffon cake is glazed with apricot jam and garnished with blueberries and slices of star fruit. The simplicity and colors of the fruit make the small cake an elegant dessert.

6
Sauces

Sauces come in endless colors and textures and are one of the easiest and most useful of garnishes. Just a simple drizzle of a colorful sauce over a dish can add richness and interest.

Most any thick liquid, store-bought or homemade, can be considered a sauce – ketchup, barbecue sauce, salad dressing, sour cream, homemade gravy, basil oil, chocolate syrup are but a few.

Pictured dessert, opposite page: You could place this lemon curd square in a napkin or a plate and eat it out of hand. Garnished, it becomes a signature dessert. The lemon square is first dusted with powdered sugar, then raspberry sauce is drizzled from a spoon across the plate and the square. Some fresh raspberries and mint leaves artfully placed complete the presentation.

Fun with Squeeze Bottles

Squeeze bottles are a trick that chefs use to make beautifully decorated plates. I keep several squeeze bottles in the refrigerator filled with a variety of sauces – sour cream, basil oil, red pepper sauce, red raspberry syrup – ready for instant garnishing. Since the bottles are readily available and inexpensive, I buy them in multiples.

Here's How:

Using them is so easy. Simply fill the bottle and squeeze. Write your initials, make a heart, draw dashes and squiggles – decorate to your heart's content. Just be sure the sauce you squeeze is flavorful and appropriate for the dish. The hole in the end of the nozzle can be enlarged with a heated ice pick.

Pictured soup left: A spicy chipotle sour cream squeezed onto cold avocado soup in a heart shape adds a pleasant zing to the soup. Chipotle peppers are smoke-dried jalapeño peppers. They come in packages and jars.

To make chipotle sour cream, purchase canned chipotle chili peppers in adobo sauce. Mince some of the pepper and add it and a bit of the adobo sauce to the sour cream. Chipotles are very hot – how much you use is a matter of taste.

Pictured opposite page: A simple cheese quesadilla (a grilled tortilla with cheese inside) is garnished with a zigzag of sour cream, cilantro sprigs, and chopped cilantro leaves. A side of guacamole is served in a lime bowl. (See the "Fruit" chapter for how to make citrus bowls.) A lime twist and a chili pepper flower occupy the center of the plate. (See the "Vegetable" chapter for how to make the pepper flower and the "Fruit" chapter for how to make a lime twist.)

---
recipe

Guacamole

1 avocado
Juice of 1/2 lime
1 garlic clove, minced
1 Tbsp. chopped
  cilantro
1 Roma or other small
  tomato, seeded and
  finely chopped
Salt and pepper to taste

1. Peel the avocado and remove the seed. (I found the easiest way to do this is to cut the avocado lengthwise into 4 sections. Pull the sections away from the seed, and discard the seed. Hold each section as you pull off the skin with your fingers.)
2. Using a fork, mash the avocado with the lime juice.
3. Add the garlic, cilantro, and tomato, stirring gently to combine. Season with salt and pepper to taste.

recipe

Fruit Sauces

A fruit sauce is a wonderful way to add color to a dessert or salad. As you will see from the recipes on the following pages, sauces are easy to make from almost any type of fruit.

The photos show how to artfully marry two fruit sauces on a plate. Soup plates or dinner or salad plates with raised rims work best for serving foods with sauces. Use a damp paper towel to clean up any drips.

Here's How:

1. **Spoon or pour** sauces on a plate. Here, two fruit sauces are placed in the quadrants of a plate with a wide, raised band.

2. **Smooth.** Use a palette knife to smooth the sauces and fill in any gaps. Gently tap the plate on the table or counter to settle the sauces.

3. **Marry.** Pull a skewer back and forth in the areas where the sauces meet to marry them.

Pictured dessert opposite: Strawberry sauce and mango sauce coexist beautifully on this plate, making a scoop of coconut sorbet a delectable dessert. A golden raspberry crowns the sorbet. Vanilla ice cream would also taste great with these two fruit sauces.

Feathered or Marbled Sauces

For this technique, you'll need two sauces in contrasting colors, a plastic squeeze bottle, and a skewer. You can use two fruit sauces or pair a dark fruit sauce (the base sauce) with heavy cream, sour cream, or creme Anglaise as the accent.

Place the base sauce on the plate and the accent sauce in the squeeze bottle. You can make lines, spirals, or any shape you like with the accent sauce. Here are two examples.

Feathered

1. **Squeeze** parallel lines of the accent sauce across the base sauce.

2. **Pull** the skewer through the lines in one direction, drawing it across the sauce.

3. **Feather** the sauce by pulling the skewer in the opposite direction.

Marbled

1. **Squeeze** the accent sauce in a spiral over the base sauce.

2. **Pull** the skewer through the accent sauce to mix and marbleize.

Hearts

This is a fun way to say "I love you" – let your food do the talking by decorating a plate with hearts made from a red fruit sauce. You will need a sauce of your choice, a plastic squeeze bottle, and a skewer. I'm using a piece of white parchment to illustrate, but you would make the heart directly on the plate, as shown on the finished dessert.

Here's How:

1. **Squeeze a dot** of sauce on the plate.

2. **Squeeze another dot** beside the first. Let them touch.

Pictured dessert: Alternating raspberry sauce hearts and candied rose petals makes a colorful border for a chocolate brownie. See "Edible Flowers" chapter to learn how to make edible candied rose petal

3. **Drag a skewer** between the two dots, pulling out a point at the bottom to make the heart.

Fruit Sauce Recipes

The basic techniques are the same for many fruit sauces. I've included recipes for some of my favorites.

Here's How:

1. **Puree.** To begin making a sauce, puree the fruit in a food processor.

2. **Strain** the pureed fruit to remove any seeds or fibers. Press the fruit in the strainer with a wooden spoon to extract as much juice as possible.

---

recipe

Fresh Fruit Sauce

You can use fresh or frozen fruit for this sauce – strawberries, raspberries, blackberries, melon, or peaches.

2 cups of fresh fruit *or* **a 20 oz. bag of frozen fruit**
1/4 cup fine dusting sugar
2 tsp. lemon juice
2 tsp. orange juice

1. Puree and strain the fruit.
2. Add sugar and stir to dissolve. Refrigerate until ready to use.

recipe

---

recipe

Mango Sauce

2 ripe mangoes
1 Tbsp. lime juice
1 Tbsp. fine dusting sugar (or to taste)

1. Place all ingredients in a food processor and puree.
2. Strain. Can be refrigerated overnight.

recipe

---

recipe

Dried Fruit Sauce

Use dried apricots, peaches, or cherries to make this sauce.

1 cup (about 4 oz.) dried fruit
2-1/2 cups water
1 cup sugar

1. Combine water, sugar, and dried fruit in a heavy saucepan. Bring mixture to a boil. Reduce heat to medium and simmer until fruit is tender, about 25 minutes.
2. Remove from heat and cool.
3. Transfer mixture to food processor and puree. If needed, add water – 1 spoonful at a time – to make a sauce-like consistency. Cover and refrigerate.

recipe

---

recipe

Cooked Fruit Sauce

This sauce has a more intense flavor than Fresh Fruit Sauce. You can use fresh or frozen strawberries, raspberries, blackberries, blueberries, or peaches.

2 cups of fresh fruit *or* **a 20 oz. bag of frozen fruit**
1/2 cup sugar
2 tsp. lemon juice
1 Tbsp. orange liqueur

1. Puree and strain the fruit.
2. Place all ingredients in a heavy saucepan. Cook over medium heat until the sugar dissolves and sauce begins to boil. Cook 1 to 2 minutes more. Allow sauce to cool in refrigerator before using.

recipe

Vegetable Coulis

A vegetable coulis is simply a puree or sauce of vegetables or herbs that does not include the peel or seeds. Use a coulis to add color and flavor to meats and fish.

You can make a coulis with fresh or frozen vegetables – peas, carrots, and spinach are especially effective because of their color and texture. Cook the vegetables just enough to soften them but not so long that they lose their vibrant color. When the vegetables are tender, plunge them in ice water to stop the cooking and set the color, then drain, puree, and strain.

If needed, add water or broth to the puree to thin it to a sauce-like consistency. Season with salt and reheat, if necessary. To lighten the color, add a tablespoon of cream.

Pictured main dish: A filet of pan-fried sea bass rests on two sauces – basil cream sauce and tomato cream coulis. Chives and salmon roe top the fish.

---

recipe

Tomato Cream Coulis

2 lb. ripe tomatoes, halved and seeded
Olive oil
1 tsp. balsamic vinegar
3 Tbsp. heavy whipping cream
Salt and pepper

1. Heat oven to 400 degrees F. Brush tomatoes with olive oil and roast in the oven, cut side down, in a baking pan for 20 minutes. Let cool. Remove the peels.
2. Place tomatoes and vinegar in food processor and puree.
3. Place in a heavy saucepan. Add cream and season with salt and pepper. Warm over low heat.

recipe

---

recipe

Basil Cream Sauce

1 cup packed fresh basil leaves
1 cup heavy whipping cream
1 small shallot, chopped
1 Tbsp. white wine vinegar
1/2 cup white wine
Salt and pepper

1. Place the wine, vinegar, and chopped shallot in a heavy saucepan. Heat and boil until liquid is reduced to a few tablespoons.
2. Add cream and cook until thickened.
3. Pour in a food processor or blender. Add basil and puree.
4. Season with salt and pepper to taste. Warm on low heat, if necessary.

recipe

Flavored Oils

When dotted or squeezed from a bottle, flavored oils make lovely garnishes for many types of foods, including salads, sandwiches, antipasto platters, cheeses, and meats. Flavored oils can also be used to dress salads.

A variety of foods can be used to flavor oils. Some of my favorites are lemon or orange zest, berries, truffles, and fresh herbs. Use extra virgin olive oil for the most intense flavor.

Here's How:

1. **Place the flavored oil** in a bowl or large measuring cup with a spout. *Option:* Pour through a strainer to remove larger bits of herb leaves.

2. **Pour** into a squeeze bottle.

3. **Squeeze** dots, lines, or dollops of oil to decorate and garnish food.

---

recipe

Herb Oil

This is a quick way to make a flavorful oil for dipping bread or dressing salads. Use the tender leaves (not the tough stems) of fresh herbs such as basil, thyme, parsley, chives, or lemon verbena. Blanching ensures your herbs will stay bright green and not become muddy green. This recipe makes slightly more than 1 cup.

1 cup olive oil
1/2 cup packed basil or parsley leaves (use 1/4 cup if using any other type of herb)
Pinch of salt

1. Wash and thoroughly dry the herbs. Blanch in 2 cups boiling water for 15 seconds. Drain immediately or remove with a slotted spoon. Plunge into ice water. Drain and squeeze dry in your hands.
2. Place the leaves in a blender along with the olive oil and salt. Process until the leaves are finely chopped. *For a more clear oil,* strain through a fine sieve.
3. Store in a tightly sealed container in the refrigerator. Unstrained herb oil will keep about 1 week in the refrigerator; strained oil will keep 2 to 3 weeks. Allow the oil to return to room temperature before use.

recipe

---

recipe

Infused Oil

Makes 2 cups.

2 cups olive oil
Food of your choice – a few sprigs of fresh rosemary, or 2 pieces of citrus zest, or 3 to 4 raspberries

1. Rinse and dry the food. Place with the oil in a heavy saucepan. Cook over low heat for about 10 minutes or until a thermometer registers 180 degrees. Remove from heat and allow to cool to room temperature.
2. Strain and place in bottles. This oil will keep in your refrigerator for several weeks.

recipe

Pictured salad or appetizer:
Serve this colorful stack as an appetizer to share or as a salad course or light lunch. Thick slices of vine ripened tomatoes and juicy cantaloupe alternate with slices of fresh mozzarella cheese. Two thin slices of prosciutto are laid like ribbons on top. Basil-infused oil is drizzled over the stack and around the plate. Sprinkle with coarse salt and pepper and garnish with a basil sprig before serving.

7

Butter & Cheese

Foods with a high fat content, such as butter and cheese, lend richness and sensual appeal to foods. Butter and cheese can take many guises – they can be shaped, molded, and curled. Just a sprinkling of grated cheese can give a dish a fine dusting of flavor.

Pictured main dish, opposite: Cheese cannelloni rest on a puddle of marinara sauce. (The sauce could be poured over the cannelloni as well.) Curls of Parmesan cheese garnish the top, while grated Parmesan cheese dusts the plate. Basil leaves add deep green color, fragrance, and flavor.

Cheese Curls

You will need a piece of imported Parmesan cheese or Romano and a swivel peeler. Have the cheese at room temperature.

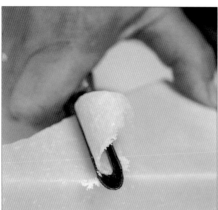

Making a cheese curl. Hold the peeler against the cheese and pull it firmly. Handle the curls carefully to retain the shape.

recipe

Grilled Corn on the Cob with Parmesan Cheese

4 ears of corn in husks
1/4 cup mayonnaise
1/4 cup soft unsalted butter
1/2 cup grated Parmesan cheese

1. Heat grill to high. Husk corn and brush off silks. Leave some of the stalk on each ear to use as a handle.
2. Mix mayonnaise and softened butter. Brush the corn with the mayonnaise/butter mixture.
3. Turn heat to medium/high. Grill corn until browned in spots – about 10 to 15 minutes, turning often.
4. Remove from grill. Brush corn with more mayonnaise/butter mixture. Roll in grated cheese.

recipe

Grated Hard Cheese

Hard cheeses such as Parmesan or Romano Pecorino can be grated with a variety of tools. My favorites are handheld microplane rasp graters.

Grating with a microplane grater.

Grating with a larger handheld flat grater – a good tool for a large piece of cheese.

Pictured opposite: Grilled Corn on the Cob with Parmesan Cheese. The grated cheese is not only the garnish but one of the the main ingredients. Give the ears a grinding of coarse pepper and sprinkle some additional cheese around the plate for the garnish. An unshucked ear of corn makes a nice accent on the plate.

Molded Cream Cheese

Cream cheese spreads look so much prettier when they are molded and coated with nuts, herbs, or spices. You can shape the cheese into balls or logs with your hands or use a bowl or other mold to create the dome shape.

Here's How:

1. **Line** a bowl or smooth-shaped mold of your choice with plastic wrap. *Alternative:* Butter the mold.

2. **Sprinkle** chopped nuts on the bottom and sides of the mold. Put more nuts on the bottom – they will spread up the sides as the cheese is pressed into the mold.

Pictured appetizer above: Two flavors of cheese spreads – blackberry and cranberry – were placed in the mold. The molded cheese is garnished with fresh cranberries and blackberries. The top is crowned with a mint sprig and a cranberry. (See the "Herbs & Spices" chapter for cheese spread recipes.)

3. **Pack** the softened cheese spread mixture in the mold, pressing the cheese to fill the mold solidly. The nuts will be pressed into the cheese as you push the cheese in place. Allow to cool in refrigerator. Unmold on a pretty plate. Gently remove the plastic wrap. Pat nuts in place, if needed.

---

recipe
Dressed Goat Cheese

Spread on French bread, crostini, or unsalted crackers.

Goat cheese log
Extra virgin olive oil
Lemon
Chives
Pepper

1. Cut a log of chilled goat cheese into rounds. Arrange on a plate.
2. Drizzle with extra virgin olive oil and garnish with lemon zest, snipped chives, and a few grinds of pepper.

recipe

Cheese Appetizer

Soft cheeses enhanced with herbs and cheese spreads with fruits, nuts, and spices are quick and easy appetizers that are proven crowd pleasers. Because most cheeses are light or neutral in color, they benefit from vibrant garnishes. See the chapter on "Herbs & Spices" for additional cheese recipes.

Pictured appetizer: Dressed Goat Cheese is a pleasant appetizer or snack.
A bundle of flowering chives decorates the plate. See opposite page for recipe.

Piped Cream Cheese

Piped cream cheese – alone or mixed with fish, finely chopped vegetables, or herbs – can be used to garnish and decorate vegetable rounds, desserts, or savory dishes. If the cream cheese is too stiff, add some cream or milk to bring it to piping consistency.

Here's How:

Squeeze. Place softened cream cheese or cream cheese spread in a pastry bag fitted with a large decorating tip. Position the tip and squeeze to release the cheese, then lift.

---
recipe

Smoked Salmon Mousse

You could use smoked trout or smoked tuna instead of the salmon.

1/2 cup smoked
  salmon
8 oz. cream cheese
2 Tbsp. soft butter
Zest of one lemon
1 Tbsp. lemon juice
1 Tbsp. chopped onion
1 Tbsp. chopped fresh
  dill
Salt and pepper to
  taste

1. Break fish into pieces.
2. Place all ingredients in a food processor and process until smooth and fluffy.

recipe

Pictured appetizer: Smoked Salmon Mousse is piped on grooved cucumber slices for a light, elegant hors d'oeuvre. Salmon roe jewels are sprinkled on top of the mousse. Lemon wedges and dill sprigs garnish the plate.

Butter Curls

There's no way around it – butter curls are more elegant than butter pats. Butter curls are easy to make. You will need a stick of chilled butter, a butter curling tool, a bowl of warm water, and a bowl of ice water.

Here's How:

1. **Prepare.** Remove the wrapper from the chilled butter. Place on a work surface. Dip the butter curling tool in warm water.

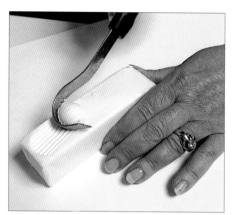

2. **Pull.** Starting at the far end of the stick of butter, pull the curling tool towards you.

3. **Chill.** Drop curls into ice water until ready to use.

Butter Balls

Herb-coated butter balls are a wonderful garnish for meats, fish, and vegetables. You will need a stick of cold butter, a melon baller, a bowl of warm water, a bowl of ice water, and the chopped herbs of your choice.

Here's How:

 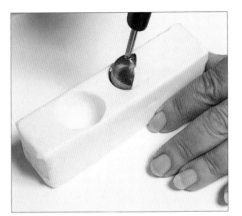 

1. **Dip** the melon baller in warm water.

2. **Press** the baller into the butter, turn, and lift out. Try for complete balls. Drop balls into ice water until you have completed all the balls you want to make.

3. **Roll in herbs.** Lift the balls and drain on a paper towel. Roll them around to remove water. Place butter balls in chopped herbs and roll to coat.

Pictured main dish: balls of herb-coated butter melt to a fragant and silky sauce when placed on a steak hot from the grill. Additional chopped herbs sprinkled on the plate create a colorful, confetti-like garnish.

8

Eggs
&
Fish

Don't limit your use of these protein foods to the main course – they, too, can be garnishes. Little tastes of salty caviar or smoky salmon add pizzazz to simple preparations. The contrasting colors of hardcooked eggs make them a natural garnish.

Pictured salad, opposite: Asian Shrimp Salad is garnished with a boiled shrimp, lemon zest, and two chive stalks. The salad was packed into a bowl-shaped mold and pushed to compress it, then covered with plastic wrap and allowed to rest in the refrigerator at least 30 minutes before unmolding. See the following page for the salad recipe.

---
recipe

Asian Shrimp Salad

Serves 2 as lunch entree. Use more or less jalapeño pepper, according to your heat preference.

6 oz. boiled shrimp
3 cups cooked rice
3/4 cup green peas
1 small carrot, shredded
2 green onions, sliced
1/4 to 1/2 jalapeño chili pepper, finely chopped
2 Tbsp. chopped cilantro
3 Tbsp. canola oil
1 tsp. freshly grated ginger root
1 tsp. grated orange zest
2 tsp. rice vinegar
Splash of toasted sesame oil
2 tsp. soy sauce
1 tsp. sugar

1. Combine ginger, orange zest, rice vinegar, sesame oil, soy sauce, canola oil, and sugar. Whisk to incorporate into a dressing.
2. Peel shrimp. Reserve 1 whole shrimp to garnish each plate. Chop remaining shrimp.
3. Mix shrimp and all other ingredients.
4. Add dressing and lightly toss.

recipe

Caviar

Caviar, or fish roe, garnishes a dish with beautiful beads of red or black. Caviar is salty with an intense flavor – so a little goes a long way.

Pictured sandwich: An open-face boiled egg sandwich might otherwise by simple country fare. Sprinkled with black caviar, it's a lunchtime luxury. Tarragon mayonnaise was used to dress the bread before topping it with the egg slices.

Pictured main dish, opposite page: Pan-fried sea bass is garnished with a bundle of snipped chives and a spoonful of salmon roe. Basil Cream Sauce and Tomato Cream Coulis sauce the dish. See the "Sauces" chapter for the recipes.

About Caviar

For more than 100 years, caviar has enjoyed a reputation as a luxury food in Western Europe and the United States. Quite simply, caviar is the eggs of large fish, specifically the eggs of the sturgeon, a large fish found in the Caspian Sea. Although the eggs of other fish, such as salmon and whitefish, are also referred to as caviar, they are more properly called "roe." Most caviar comes from Russia, Iran, Scandinavia, or the United States.

Each variety of sturgeon caviar has a distinctive flavor and texture. Beluga's large granules, for example, are pearly to dark gray with a smooth texture and delicate flavor. The taste of Oestra is often described as "nutty." Its granules are smaller than those of beluga and are golden brown in color. Sevruga has tiny granules and a creamy texture. Which type of caviar is best is a matter of personal taste.

Salmon roe has large, red-orange granules; its taste is sometimes described as "buttery." Whitefish roe is golden in color and mild in taste. You will sometimes find whitefish roe colored with beets (deep red) or wasabi (green) or other colors.

Storage: Because caviar is highly perishable, it must be kept refrigerated until it's eaten, and it should be stored in the coldest part of your refrigerator. Unopened, fresh caviar will last 2 to 3 weeks. Pasteurized caviar, unopened, will last 3 to 4 months. Opened caviar should be consumed within 1 week.

Handling: Traditionally, caviar is served with tiny spoons made of mother-of-pearl, carved horn, or gold because silver, stainless steel, or other metal utensils will react with the caviar, imparting an undesirable metallic taste. Spoons made with other non-reactive materials, such as glass, plastic, or wood, will not affect the taste and so are appropriate to use.

Smoked Salmon Rose

Colorful slices of smoked salmon can be shaped into elegant roses. To make them, you will need cold smoked salmon slices, a skewer, and some sprigs of dill.

Here's How:

1. **Fold.** Take a slice of salmon and fold it in half lengthwise.

2. **Coil.** Wind the strip to form a loose spiral.

3. **Pinch** the base to compress and place on a surface, folded edge down.

4. **Arrange.** Use the skewer to separate each layer to form the petals.

5. **Decorate** with dill sprigs.

Pictured breakfast, opposite page:
Quiche is topped with creme fraiche, a salmon rose, and dill sprigs. Capers decorate the plate.

Eggs

Hard-cooked eggs can be chopped, riced, diced, sliced, and quartered to create beautiful garnishes for vegetables, salads, and meats.

To hard-cook eggs, place them in a large pot of cold water. Place on medium heat and allow them to come to a boil. Boil gently for 12-13 minutes. Remove from water and place in a pot of cold water. Allow to cool before peeling. Store cooked eggs in refrigerator for 3 to 4 days. TIP: Don't overcook eggs – boiling too long will cause the yolk to have a green halo.

Riced: Eggs can be put through a ricer to create fine pieces.

Sliced: An egg slicer is a handy gadget, but not necessary to slice eggs thinly. (You can use a knife instead.)

Quartered: Egg quarters are easy to cut with a sharp knife. Dip knife into hot water before each slice to keep yellow from sticking and crumbling.

— *recipe* —

Sauteed Spinach

Wash a bag or bundle of spinach carefully to remove all the sandy grit. Shake off excess moisture. Thinly slice 2 cloves of garlic. Heat 2 Tbsp. olive oil in a skillet. Add spinach, heaping it to overflowing in the skillet. Immediately add the sliced garlic and sprinkle with salt and pepper. Use tongs to toss the spinach in the skillet as it cooks. Cook just until slightly wilted – about 3 minutes.

— *recipe* —

Pictured vegetable dish opposite page: Chopped hard-cooked eggs garnish a plate of sauteed spinach.

Pictured sandwich: Tuna salad sandwich on whole wheat is a lunchtime regular. To take it up a notch, garnish with egg slices. Add squiggles of mayonnaise, dill sprigs, and capers.

Pictured appetizer: Deviled eggs are standard picnic and potluck fare; be sure the ones you bring make the best impression. Here, egg yolks are combined with mayonnaise and other seasonings, then piped into the egg white halves. A bed of fresh herb sprigs cushions the surface and keeps the eggs from rolling and sliding on the plate. A sprinkling of spice – paprika, cayenne, smoked paprika, or curry powder, for example – adds a burst of flavor. Olives and capers are randomly strewn for a casual garnish.

9
Edible Flowers

Using flowers as a garnish is a wonderful way to bring the beauty of your garden to the table. Popular flowers to use as garnishes include roses, pansies, violets, nasturtiums, and lavender.

Most herb flowers are safe to eat – they taste slightly milder than the herb's leaves. Rose petals add an incredibly romantic look to desserts and an exotic flavor. Pansies are so colorful they almost steal the show. They are particularly pretty when used on white foods such as goat cheese or on a slice of cheesecake. Nasturtiums' slightly peppery taste makes them a tasty salad garnish. Their bright orange or yellow color brings greens to life. Lavender may be my favorite. The color and fragrance is so heady I nearly swoon with pleasure at the sight, smell, and taste of this flower.

It's very important to select flowers with care. First, choose only those that you are positive are edible, and eat only the petals. (Herbs are an exception – you can eat the stems and buds.) Second, make sure no pesticides or herbicides have been used on the flowers – this means never use flowers from florists, nurseries, or garden centers. Flowers you grow yourself without pesticides, herbicides, or chemical fertilizers are the safest flowers to eat. You may also be able to find organic growers who sell flowers – ask at farmer's markets.

Flowers are very perishable and should be used the day they are picked. They lose flavor and texture quite rapidly.

Popular Edible Flowers

Basil flowers
Chive and garlic blossoms
Dandelions
Lavender flowers and buds
Nasturtiums
Orchids - Dendrobium varieties and vanilla orchid
Pansies
Rose petals
Squash blossoms
Violets

Pictured appetizer opposite: This appetizer plate couldn't be prettier. Goat cheese rounds are decorated with pansies, violets, and herbs that have been adhered to the cheese with gelatin. When sealed with the gelatin, the flowers will maintain their just-picked appearance for several days. More flowers, herbs, and lemon zest decorate the plate. For instructions on how to adhere the flowers to the cheese, see page 107.

Candied Flower Petals

Candied flower petals are brushed with egg white, then dusted with sugar and allowed to dry. If the weather is damp or humid, you can aid the drying process by putting the sugared flower petals on a baking sheet and placing them in an oven heated to 300 degrees F. for 10 minutes.

Because the egg white is not cooked, use only pasteurized eggs.

Here's How:

1. **Beat** an egg white until slightly frothy.

2. **Brush.** Use a small brush to apply the egg white to the flower petal.

3. **Dust.** Place the flower petal in a bowl of fine sugar. Sprinkle more sugar on top. Place on a rack to dry.

Pictured dessert: A small cheesecake is glazed with rose petal jelly and topped with candied rose petals. See the "Fruit" chapter for more information on glazing with jelly. Mint leaves garnish the base of the cheesecake.

About sugar: Use regular, fine granulated sugar or sanding sugar which has larger granules and add more sparkle than regular sugar.

Edible Flowers

Pictured dessert above: Store-bought cupcakes from a bakery or supermarket are dressed up for a party. The cupcakes were put in fresh paper baking cups; fresh rose petals were placed between the cupcake and the paper cup. Candied violets decorate the tops of the cupcakes. Candied rose petals are scattered on the platter.

Adhering Flowers to Cheese *See photo on page 105.*

1. **Brush.** Dissolve some plain gelatin in warm water in a small bowl. Brush liquid gelatin over the top of the cheese.

2. **Arrange** the flowers and herbs on the cheese, pressing them lightly into the liquid gelatin.

3. **Seal.** Brush more gelatin over the top to seal.

10
Chocolate

Nothing tastes better than chocolate, and now scientists tell us chocolate is loaded with antioxidants and – in moderation, of course – eating chocolate is good for us (as if we needed encouragement).

Don't be scared of using chocolate as a garnish because you think it's difficult to work with. With a little attention, you can become skilled at chocolate crafting, and your friends will think you quite the chocolate artist. For best results, avoid working with chocolate on hot, humid days.

Pictured dessert opposite: Chocolate curls were created with a vegetable peeler to decorate a miniature (4″ diameter) chocolate mousse cake.

How to Melt Chocolate

Once you learn to melt chocolate correctly, you can make any garnish in this chapter. The two things to remember are to melt chocolate over hot, not boiling water; and to not overheat the chocolate – if you do, it will "seize up" or "tighten," and you won't be able to do a thing with it.

Start with the best quality chocolate you can find – one with at least 35 percent cocoa solids. The higher the percentage of cocoa solids the better. Choose semisweet or bittersweet dark chocolate; chocolate coating won't do.

You will need a double boiler with a clean, dry top pan or a dry heat-resistant bowl that will fit snugly over another pan. You will also need a clean, dry wooden spoon. The water in the bottom pan of the double boiler should not touch the bottom of the top pan or the bowl, if you're using a bowl. Do not try to melt more than one pound of chocolate at a time.

Here's How:

1. **Chop** the chocolate by placing the chocolate block on a cutting board and using a chef's knife to cut off small pieces. Put the chopped chocolate in the top of the double boiler or the heat-resistant bowl.

2. **Melt.** Heat water in the bottom of the double boiler or a saucepan. When the water begins to boil, remove the pan from the heat, put the top of the double boiler or a bowl that contains the chopped chocolate in place, and begin stirring. Stir until the chocolate is melted. Do not allow any steam to get to the chocolate.

Pictured dessert opposite page: A 4″ chocolate cake is frosted with chocolate ganache. The side of the cake is garnished with finely chopped nuts. Chocolate leaves and red raspberries crown the top.

Chocolate Leaves

Chocolate leaves are a beautiful garnish. You will need bittersweet or semisweet chocolate, a small brush, a double boiler, and clean and dry thick leaves that are non-poisonous, such as rose leaves. A piece of parchment makes a good work surface.

Here's How:

1. **Brush** melted chocolate on the veined undersides of clean, dry leaves. Coat thickly and completely.

2. **Let set.** If it is a warm or humid day, you may need to slide the leaves into the refrigerator for 30 to 45 minutes to allow chocolate to harden.

3. **Peel** away the leaves, starting at the stem ends.

Chocolate Curls

Chocolate curls are a beautiful garnish for any chocolate dessert. There are two ways to make chocolate curls.

Here's How:

1. **Pour** melted chocolate on a piece of marble.

2. **Spread and smooth** the chocolate with a spatula.

3. **Push** a flat-ended metal spatula against the chocolate to curl it.

OR: Simply pull a vegetable peeler across a block of high quality chocolate to make curls.

Pictured dessert, opposite page: A flourless chocolate cake, baked in a cupcake pan, gets its height from two freeform chocolate ovals. The cake sits in a pool of vanilla cream decorated with swirls of chocolate sauce applied from a squeeze bottle. A slice of star fruit and a couple of raspberries are the fruits of desire.

Chocolate Shapes

Piped squiggles of melted chocolate will set up to form fun shapes for decorating desserts. You will need a pastry bag fitted with a plain decorating tip or a plastic food storage bag, melted dark semisweet chocolate, and a non-stick surface such as parchment paper. Using a plastic bag means no messy cleanup – you just toss the empty bag when you're finished. If you use a plastic bag, you won't need a tip – simply make an opening by snipping off a tiny bit off one bottom corner with scissors.

Here's How:

1. **Fill** the bag with melted chocolate.

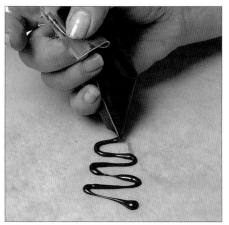

2. **Pipe** chocolate into desired shapes on a non-stick surface. Allow chocolate to set up. Chill in refrigerator if needed. Peel up from paper.

11
Garnishes for Sweets

Desserts are fun to garnish. In this chapter you'll see a variety of creative ways to decorate desserts using sugar, nuts, food-safe markers, and gold leaf, to name a few.

Powdered Sugar

A sprinkle of powdered sugar instantly provides the finishing embellishment that turns plain cake or pastry to fancy. For ease of use, place the powdered sugar in a shaker with holes that are a little larger than the holes in a salt or pepper shaker, or use a sifter.

Stenciling with Powdered Sugar

To take the embellishment a step further, use a stencil to add a design to a plain cake with powdered sugar. You'll find a wide variety of stencils at crafts stores or stores where cake decorating supplies are sold. Paper doilies also make an interesting design on a cake. Or try cutting a simple shape from a piece of parchment.

Here's How:

Stencil. Simply place the stencil or doily on the cake and sprinkle a thick layer of the sugar. Lift off stencil, being careful not to spill any of the sugar left on the stencil.

Pictured dessert: A powdered sugar heart was stenciled on a brownie cutout. The plate is decorated with candied rose petals (see the "Edible Flowers" chapter) and raspberry sauce hearts (see the "Sauces" chapter).

To make the brownie cutout, spread brownie mix in a jelly roll pan and bake to create a thin layer. Let cool, then use biscuit cutters or cookie cutters to make shapes. (For this example, I used a round biscuit cutter.) TIP: Don't throw away those extra brownie pieces – save them for nibbling or mix them into soft vanilla ice cream to make your own signature ice cream flavor (and another delicious dessert).

Pastry Bag Decorating

Pastry tube decorating is a lot more fun without the tiresome task of cleaning the bag, and you can easily make disposable pastry bags with parchment paper. Then all you need are some decorating tips (which can be cleaned in the dishwasher). *Option:* If you just want to pipe a straight line, simply snip off the end of the paper tube to create a hole.

Here's How:

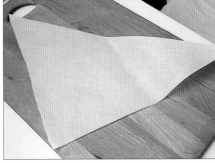

1. **Cut** a triangle of parchment.

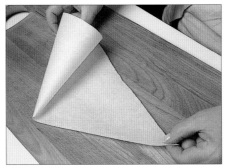

2. **Roll** the triangle into a cone shape.

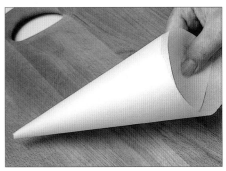

3. Make sure the pointed end of the cone is rolled tightly, without a hole in it.

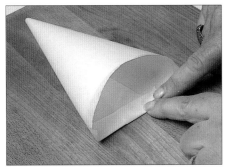

4. **Fold** the flap on the open end of the cone to secure the cone shape.

5. **Snip** a hole in the pointed end of the cone that's large enough to accommodate a tip.

6. **Drop in** a decorating tip, if you're using one. (See the option above.)

7. **Fill** the cone with icing, melted chocolate, softened cream cheese, or other food.

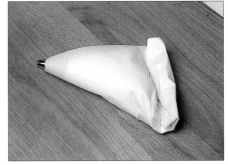

8. **Push** the food into the tip by folding the top of the cone. Squeeze the bag to allow the food to emerge from the tip.

Pictured dessert: Piped white chocolate personalizes this dessert plate and decorates a rich oatmeal raisin chocolate cookie. Add ice cream, caramel sauce, and golden raspberries to create a memorable dessert.

116

Colored Coconut

Shreds of coconut can obscure a less-than-perfect icing job. Coconut also looks great sprinkled over fruit cups or ice cream. On special holidays or for children's parties, colored coconut will make everyone smile.

Pictured dessert: Colored coconut shreds create a nest for jellybeans on an Easter cupcake.

Here's How:

1. **Place** shredded coconut in a plastic bag.

2. **Add** one drop of food coloring. (Really, that's all it takes!)

3. **Massage** the bag to mix the food coloring into the coconut.

Cake Decorating Toppings

Cake decorations from the store can be tasteful and elegant if you use them with discretion. In the photo *below,* one tiny gold dragee adds a touch of elegance to a fudgy brownie that's served on a golden plate and garnished with an edible flower. Use tweezers to ensure exact placement.

Burnt Sugar Brittle

Cooked sugar can be drizzled on a non-stick surface to create a beautiful transparent shape for decorating desserts. This works best on a cool, dry day.

Here's How:

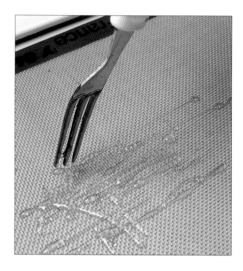

1. **Mix** 1 cup of sugar and 1/2 cup of water in a heavy saucepan. Stir over medium heat until the sugar dissolves, making a syrup.
2. **Boil.** Increase the heat and bring to a boil. Boil until the syrup is a pale golden color. As the syrup boils, use a wet pastry brush to brush down the sides of the pan and dissolve any sugar crystals that form on the sides of the pan.
3. **Cool.** Remove the pan from the heat. Let the syrup cool until it is thick enough to fall from the tines of a fork. TIP: Whip the syrup with the fork to hasten the cooling process and incorporate air into the sugar mixture. If the syrup gets too thick, it can be reheated.
4. **Dip and wave.** Working over a non-stick surface such as a piece of parchment paper, dip the fork in the thickened syrup and wave it back and forth, allowing it to form strings and ribbons.
5. **Peel up.** Allow the syrup to harden. Peel the shape from the paper.

Food Safe Markers

Let the kids have fun decorating their food and plates with food safe markers. Find them where cake decorating supplies are sold.

Pictured dessert opposite page: A caramel flan is enhanced with airy pieces of burnt sugar brittle.

Chopped Nuts

Chopped nuts add flavor and texture to foods and, as the saying goes, they can "cover a multitude of sins." For best results, use a small handheld chopper – the chopper holds the nuts so the pieces don't end up all over the counter. Although it might seem like a good idea, don't use a food processor for chopping nuts – it can create uneven pieces and extract too much oil from the nuts, making a sticky mess.

Chopping nuts in a handheld chopper.

---
recipe

Chocolate Truffles

My holiday indulgence is making chocolate truffles. I roll some in chopped nuts and others in cocoa powder.

8 oz. high quality, semi-sweet chocolate
1/2 cup heavy cream
2 Tbsp. orange or raspberry liqueur

1. Chop the chocolate and set aside.
2. Bring the cream to a boil in a heavy saucepan. Remove from heat and allow to cool 30 seconds.
3. Add chocolate to pan. Stir until the chocolate is melted.
4. Add liqueur and stir.
5. Allow to cool on the counter about 30 minutes, then cover the pan loosely with foil or plastic wrap and place in the refrigerator until firm.
6. Shape into balls and roll in the topping of your choice.

recipe

Truffles

1. **Scoop.** Use a melon baller dipped in hot water to scoop out a perfect ball.

2. **Coat.** Roll in chopped nuts, pressing the nuts into the surface.

3. **Or** roll in cocoa powder.

Gold Leaf

Small amounts of gold are perfectly edible, and gold leaf adds an undeniable touch of elegance to any dessert. Be sure to use 24 carat pure gold leaf – it's very thin and floats like a feather. Do not use imitation gold metal leaf. Sticky desserts like this pecan tart hold the leaf and give the best results.

Here's How:

Float a sheet of gold leaf onto the surface of your dessert, holding the leaf in one hand and using a skewer in the other hand to touch the leaf to the surface. Pull away, allowing uneven pieces of the leaf to stick to the surface.

Marzipan

Marzipan is an edible confection of ground almonds and sugar that has a clay-like texture. Making fruits, vegetables, and flowers from marzipan is like modeling with clay – marzipan can be formed into anything your imagination can dream up.

Marzipan can be rolled into a sheet with a rolling pin and draped over a cake or cut into shapes with cookie cutters. It also can be used as a filling for cakes and pastry, chocolate candies, or dried fruits.

You can buy marzipan in ready-to-use packages. It will stay fresh for weeks in the refrigerator and can be frozen for months. Keep the marzipan tightly wrapped to prevent it from drying out.

It can be colored with cocoa (to make a deep brown) or with liquid, paste, or gel food coloring. Paste colors are the most intense – add just a little at a time until you achieve the colors you want. After coloring and shaping, the pieces can be shaded with additional liquid or gel food coloring.

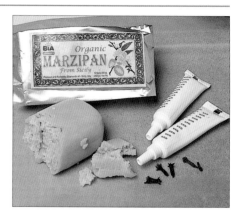

The photos that follow show how to make a marzipan pear.

Here's How:

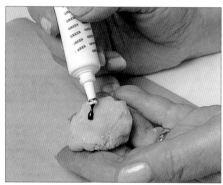

1. **Knead** the chilled marzipan until it is soft enough to shape. Work on a cool surface such as a marble slab or a tray that has been refrigerated so that you don't overheat the marzipan.

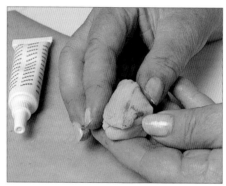

2. **Add** food coloring to the mixture and knead to color the piece.

3. **Shape** the item.

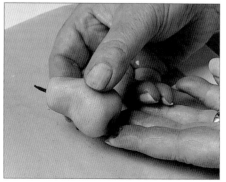

4. **Push** dried cloves into the fruit shape for a stem and a bud end.

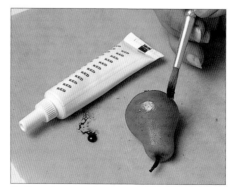

5. **Brush** on gel or liquid food coloring to shade and highlight the item.

6. *Optional:* **Coat** with a clear vegetable glaze if you wish for your shapes to look shiny. You can buy the glaze at stores that sell cake decorating supplies.

Pictured dessert cake: This small cake, 4″ in diameter and decorated with four pieces of marzipan fruit, is the perfect size for feeding four guests at teatime – simply cut the cake in fourths and serve each piece with a marzipan fruit.

Making the Marzipan Fruit

The *orange* was colored with orange paste food coloring; the texture was created by rolling the ball over a fine grater. A clove was pushed into the stem end.

The *banana* was colored with yellow paste coloring and shaded with brown liquid color. I used the tip of a brush to add brown sugar spots.

The *peach* was colored with yellow paste coloring with a tiny bit of orange paste added. I used the shaft of a skewer to press the indentation and shaded it with light pink coloring. A clove was pushed in the top for a stem.

The *pear* was colored with green coloring. Light pink was used to add the blush. Cloves were pressed in the blossom and stem ends.

All the pieces were glazed with vegetable glaze and sprinkled with edible glitter.

Cookie & Candy Toppings

Crushed hard candies and crushed cookies are easy garnishes that turn plain into pretty.

Here's How:

One way: Place candy or cookies in a bag and crush with a rolling pin.

Another way: Use a chopper to crush the candy or cookies.

Pictured desserts: Crushed chocolate mint wafer cookies jazz up chocolate pudding served in a clear glass and topped with whipped cream. A mint leaf adds a spark of color. Crushed red-and-white peppermints turn a plain brownie into a Christmas treat. Using a mint sprig as a garnish continues the plate's festive green and red color scheme.

Metric Conversion Chart

Inches to Millimeters and Centimeters

Inches	MM	CM	Inches	MM	CM
1/8	3	.3	2	51	5.1
1/4	6	.6	3	76	7.6
3/8	10	1.0	4	102	10.2
1/2	13	1.3	5	127	12.7
5/8	16	1.6	6	152	15.2
3/4	19	1.9	7	178	17.8
7/8	22	2.2	8	203	20.3
1	25	2.5	9	229	22.9
1-1/4	32	3.2	10	254	25.4
1-1/2	38	3.8	11	279	27.9
1-3/4	44	4.4	12	305	30.5

Yards to Meters

Yards	Meters	Yards	Meters
1/8	.11	3	2.74
1/4	.23	4	3.66
3/8	.34	5	4.57
1/2	.46	6	5.49
5/8	.57	7	6.40
3/4	.69	8	7.32
7/8	.80	9	8.23
1	.91	10	9.14
2	1.83		

Index

Index